NEW
Beginnings

NEW
Beginnings

365 Daily Meditations
and Affirmations
for Inspiration

Becca Anderson

Mango Publishing
CORAL GABLES

Cover Design: Roberto Nunez
Layout & Design: Carmen Fortunato

For permission requests, please contact the publisher at:
Mango Publishing Group
2850 S Douglas Road, 2nd Floor
Coral Gables, FL 33134 USA
info@mango.bz

For special orders, quantity sales, course adoptions and corporate sales, please email the publisher at sales@mango.bz. For trade and wholesale sales, please contact Ingram Publisher Services at customer.service@ingramcontent.com or +1.800.509.4887.

New Beginnings: 365 Daily Meditations and Affirmations for Inspiration

Library of Congress Cataloging-in-Publication number: 2020950828
ISBN: (print) 978-1-64250-537-5, (ebook) 978-1-64250-538-2
BISAC category code OCC019000, BODY, MIND & SPIRIT / Inspiration & Personal Growth

Printed in the United States of America

Table of Contents

Introduction:

Open Your Heart to the Wisdom Inside You

Dear Reader,

I created this book of prayers for both you and me. The ups and downs we have seen throughout the world in recent times caused many of us to look at life with fresh perspectives. Upon rising every morning, how we spiritually greet each day could very well determine how our future unfolds. In turn, folks everywhere have decided to seek out new paths in hopes of uncovering their true purposes in life. Starting out each day with a special blessing or prayer is critical to such a journey.

Regardless of our age, livelihood, or family situation, a new beginning might mean a short detour along our current path, or it could take you in a completely new direction. Some people make changes because they are unhappy with something small in their life; others do so because they believe that they need a complete overhaul. Sometimes advice is coming from all sorts of people in every direction, but the important thing is to find the path that's best for us—the path that makes us the happiest. Uncovering the necessary changes is not easy, as it's critical for us to look inside ourselves to find the true intentions of our souls.

Take a moment to think about what you want in your life and why you want to make this particular change. Allow your heart to open to the wisdom that already lives inside you. How are you going to make it happen? Do you have the desire and the courage to see it the whole way through? Sometimes these changes are scary. Some of us might need to make one or more sacrifices—mentally, physically, or even financially. It might require stepping out of your comfort zone in order to find the path to your true potential.

Perhaps the most important tools in facing these journeys are inspiration and motivation. Some folks may be able to muster the courage to face these challenges alone, but most of us find we need the support of other people. If you dig deep enough, there is unlimited wisdom available courtesy of the world's most famous leaders, poets, writers, and scientists. More times than not, a few powerful words are all the motivation you might need. That was the main vision behind the creation of this book—providing you with a daily message in hopes of keeping you moving in the right direction.

It's time to reclaim your life and rediscover the true joy of your existence.

Making a change or starting over isn't the worst thing you can do.

Giving up is.

January

A New Lease on Life

"The person who removes a mountain begins
by carrying away small stones."

—CHINESE PROVERB

"Bravery is being terrified and doing it anyway."

—LAURELL K. HAMILTON

"It always seems impossible until it is done."

—NELSON MANDELA

"You must do the thing you think you cannot do."

—ELEANOR ROOSEVELT

"I came, I saw, I conquered."

—JULIUS CAESAR

"Life is what we make it, always has been, always will be."

—GRANDMA MOSES

Change

Change will not come if we wait for some other person,
or if we wait for some other time.
We are the ones we've been waiting for.
We are the change that we seek.

—*Barack Obama*

Tiny Prayer

May you make plans to regularly step away for several
moments a day,
knowing that the news is out there,
that the fight is out there,
that the sustaining of a movement is bigger than you,
that it requires you to take care of your body and soul,
which means breathing into the horrors you already know,
taking a break from ingesting more,
and trusting your communities to continually balance the work,
staggering participation so that the collective spirit moves,
even during the moments when you are at necessary rest.

Amen.

—*Micah Bucey (2020)*

Prayer for Peace

May I become at all times, both now and forever
A protector for those without protection
A guide for those who have lost their way
A ship for those with oceans to cross
A bridge for those with rivers to cross
A sanctuary for those in danger
A lamp for those without light
A place of refuge for those who lack shelter
And a servant to all in need.

—*Buddhist Prayer of Peace*

God Grant Me Grace to Be My Best Self

Give us the strength it takes
to listen rather than to judge,
to trust rather than to fear,
to try again and again
to make peace even when peace eludes us.

We ask, O God, for the grace
to be our best selves.
We ask for the vision
to be builders of the human community
rather than its destroyers.
We ask for the humility as a people
to understand the fears and hopes of other peoples.

We ask for the love it takes
to bequeath to the children of the world to come
more than the failures of our own making.
We ask for the heart it takes
to care for all the peoples.
For You, O God, have been merciful to us.

For You, O God, have been patient with us.
For You, O God, have been gracious to us.
And so may we be merciful
and patient
and gracious
and trusting
with these others whom you also love.
This we ask through Jesus,
the one without vengeance in his heart.
This we ask forever and ever.

Amen.

—*Benedictine Sisters' Prayer for World Peace*

Every Tomorrow Is a Vision of Hope

Look to this day,
For yesterday is but a dream,
And tomorrow is only a vision,
But today, well lived,
Makes every yesterday a dream of happiness,
And every tomorrow a vision of hope.
Look well, therefore, to this day.

—*Kalidasa, from ancient Sanskrit*

The Only Thing That Matters

I do not think that the measure of a civilization
is how tall its buildings of concrete are,
but rather how well its people have learned to relate
to their environment and fellow man.

—Sun Bear, Chippewa Medicine Man

Bloom

I want to tell you
about the sunflower I found
on the sidewalk yesterday.
It is wilting and curled and gorgeous
and knows it.
I want to age like that,
never forgetting my own beauty,
never forgetting how to say bloom.

—Anna Voelker

Today I Purpose to Love

My life will shine
As the morning sings
I walk in liberty
Bound in true dreams
Manifested promises
Chase my forward motion
A covered path before me
The fruits of my hoping
The fruits of my living

Today I purpose to love

My love will speak
With the sound of grace
Merciful within mercy
The works of my faith
Smiles of overflowing
Inspire my giving

Abundance of joy as rain
The fruits of my living

—Michael John Faciane

Mother Teresa's Prayer for Purpose

Make us worthy, Lord, to serve our fellow men
throughout the world who live and die in poverty and hunger.
Give them through our hands this day their daily bread,
and by our understanding love, give peace and joy.

—Mother Teresa

Live Each Day As If It Is Your Last

As my life today
has been determined by the way I lived my yesterday,
So my tomorrow is being determined by the way
I live my today.

—Ralph Waldo Trine

Joy and Good Will and Serenity

As you cannot have a sweet and wholesome abode
unless you admit the air and sunshine freely into your rooms,
so a strong body
and a bright, happy, or serene countenance
can only result from the free admittance into the mind
of thoughts of joy and good will and serenity.

—James Allen

Discover What Is Truly Important in Life

In humility is the greatest freedom.
As long as you have to defend the imaginary self
that you think is important, you lose your peace of heart.
As soon as you compare that shadow
with the shadows of other people, you lose all joy,
because you have begun to trade in unrealities
and there is no joy in things that do not exist.

—Thomas Merton, 1961

What You Can Rise From

You may encounter many defeats,
but you must not be defeated.
In fact, it may be necessary to encounter the defeats,
so you can know who you are,
what you can rise from,
how you can still come out of it.

—Maya Angelou

Everything Will Be New Again

As he sat by the river,
the eyes of his understanding began to be opened;
not that he saw any vision,
but he understood and learnt many things,
both spiritual matters and matters of faith and of scholarship,
and this with so great an enlightenment
that everything seemed new to him.

—*St. Ignatius of Loyola, sixteenth century*

Our Spirits Are Being Renewed Every Day

We are pressed on every side by troubles,
but we are not crushed and broken.
We are perplexed, but we don't give up and quit.
That is why we never give up.
Though our bodies are dying,
our spirits are being renewed every day.
For our present troubles are quite small
and won't last very long.
Yet they produce for us an immeasurably
great glory that will last forever!

—*2 Corinthians 4:8–18*

A New Start

Let there be respect for the earth,
Peace for its people,
Love in our lives,
Delight in the good,
Forgiveness for past wrongs
And from now on, a new start.

—*Reverend Peter Trow*

Rediscovery

Instead of saying, "I'm damaged, I'm broken,
I have trust issues,"
say, "I'm healing, I'm rediscovering myself, I'm starting over."

—*Horacio Jones*

Thou Art My Guide and Refuge

O God!
Refresh and gladden my spirit.
Purify my heart.
Illumine my powers.
I lay all my affairs in Thy hands.
Thou art my Guide and my Refuge.
I will no longer be sorrowful and grieved;
I will be a happy and joyful being.
O God! I will no longer be full of anxiety,
nor will I let trouble harass me.

I will not dwell on the unpleasant things of life.
O God! Thou art more friend to me than I am to myself.
I dedicate myself to Thee, O Lord.

—*Baha'i Prayers, Abdu'l-Bahá*

Create in Me a Pure Heart

Create in me a pure heart, O God,
and renew a steadfast spirit within me.

Do not cast me from your presence
or take your Holy Spirit from me.

Restore to me the joy of salvation
and grant me a willing spirit, to sustain me.

—*Psalm 51:10–12 (King David)*

Every New Beginning

Every new beginning
comes from some other
beginning's end.

—*Seneca*

Live Life

Live life when you have it.
Life is a splendid gift.
There is nothing small about it.

—*Florence Nightingale*

Glory

Look at everything as though you were seeing it for the first or the last time, then your time on earth will be filled with glory.

—*Betty Smith*

Walk with Us

Creator God,
at the start
of this New Year,
when thoughts turn again
to beginnings,
starting afresh,
new leaves
and turning skeletons
free from cupboards,
be with us
as we gaze into the distance
of fresh mission grounds,
of hopes and dreams,
opportunities for service,
challenges
and uncertainties.
Take our fears
and turn them into strengths.
Take our lack of faith
and empower us,

through the Spirit
who breathes life into this world,
whose presence is reflected
in the icy chill
of winter's breath,
as well as the comforting warmth
of a summer breeze.
Walk with us into this New Year
of opportunity.

—*John Birch*

Grant Us the Confidence

Grant us the confidence, Lord
to step out in faith and become
the people we are meant to be,
unapologetic in our love for you,
wanting to be change-makers,
bringers of hope, love, and grace
into an unbelieving world
that has no faith but in itself,
is almost blind and cannot see
that all it seeks is found in you.
Grant us the confidence, Lord
to step out in faith and become
the people we are meant to be.

—*United Methodist Prayer*

For all whose journey
has only just begun,
who tread carefully
and heavy laden
along unfamiliar paths,
seeking guidance
from fellow travelers,
fearful of losing their way,
speed their journey, Lord,
keep them from harm,
and bring them safely
into their promised land,
your Kingdom, where,
at last unburdened,
they might find their rest in you.

—*Celtic Prayer*

The Miracle

Though I was dwelling in a prison house,
My soul was wandering by the carefree stream
Through fields of green with gold eyed daisies strewn,
And daffodils and sunflower cavaliers.
And near me played a little brown-eyed child,
A winsome creature God alone conceived,
"Oh, little friend," I begged. "Give me a flower
That I might bear it to my lonely cell."

He plucked a dandelion, an ugly bloom,
But tenderly he placed it in my hand,
And in his eyes I saw the sign of love.
T'was then the dandelion became a rose.

—Fenton Johnson

Seize the Opportunity

There is an island of opportunity
in the middle of every difficulty.

—Alcoholics Anonymous

The Measure of Success

I have learned that success is to be measured
not so much by the position that one has reached in life
as by the obstacles which one has overcome
while trying to succeed.

—Booker T. Washington

Seeing Life as an Adventure

Do not stop thinking of life as an adventure.
You have no security unless you can live bravely,
excitingly, imaginatively;
unless you can choose a challenge instead of competence.

—Eleanor Roosevelt

Putting on the New Self

You were taught, with regard to your former way of life,
to put off your old self, which is being corrupted by its
deceitful desires;
to be made new in the attitude of your minds;
and to put on the new self,
created to be like God in true righteousness and holiness.

—Ephesians 4:22–24

The Greatest Glory

"The greatest glory in living lies not in never falling,
but in rising every time we fall.

—Nelson Mandela

February

Straight from the Heart

"A true friend never gets in your way unless
you happen to be going down."

—ARNOLD H. GLASOW

"The most beautiful discovery true friends make is that
they can grow separately without growing apart."

—ELISABETH FOLEY

"Friendship is the only cement that will
ever hold the world together."

—WOODROW T. WILSON

"A friend knows the song in my heart and
sings it to me when my memory fails."

—DONNA ROBERTS

"One loyal friend is worth ten thousand relatives."

—EURIPIDES

"A friendship that can end never really began."

—PUBLILIUS SYRUS

Every Little Kindness Matters

Every little kindness
and caring thing
we do
for peace
and safety
for all living things
matters.

—*Charlene Costanzo*

Eternal Love for All in the World

For as long as space endures
And for as long as living beings remain
Until then may I too abide
To dispel the misery of the world.

—*Shantideva, India, eighth century*

There Is a Love That Never Fails

There is an Eye that never sleeps,
beneath the wind of night.
There is an Ear that never shuts,
When sinks the beam of light.
There is an Arm that never tires,
When human strength gives way.
There is a Love that never fails,
When earthly loves decay.

—*George Mathewson*

To Those I Love

If I should ever leave you
To go along the silent way, grieve not,
Nor speak of me with tears, but laugh and talk
Of me as if I were beside you there.
(I'd come—I'd come, could I but find a way!
But would not tears and grief be barriers?)
And when you hear a song or see a bird
I loved, please do not let the thought of me
Be sad...for I am loving you just as I always have.
You were so good to me!
There are so many things I wanted still
To do—so many things to say to you.
Remember that I did not fear. It was
Just leaving you that was so hard to face.
We cannot see beyond. But this I know:
I loved you so—`twas heaven here with you!

—*Isla Paschal Richardson*

Give Your Hearts in Love

You were born together, and together
you shall be forevermore.
You shall be together when white
wings of death scatter your days.
Aye, you shall be together even in the silent memory of God.
But let there be spaces in your togetherness,
And let the winds of the heavens dance between you.
Love one another but make not a bond of love:
Let it rather be a moving sea between the shores of your souls.
Fill each other's cup, but drink not from one cup.
Give one another of your bread, but
eat not from the same loaf.
Sing and dance together and be joyous,
but let each one of you be alone,
Even as the strings of a lute are alone though
they quiver with the same music.
Give your hearts, but not into each other's keeping.
For only the hand of Life can contain your hearts.
And stand together, yet not too near together:
For the pillars of the temple stand apart,
And the oak tree and the cypress grow not in each
other's shadow.

—*Kahlil Gibran*

Know There Is Love in the World

At the center of the universe is a
loving heart that continues to beat
and that wants the best for every person.
Anything we can do to help foster
the intellect and spirit and emotional growth
of our fellow human beings, that is our job.
Those of us who have this particular vision
must continue against all odds.
Life is for service.

—Fred Rogers, Mr. Rogers' Neighborhood

Peace in the Home, Peace in the Heart

If there is to be peace in the world,
There must be peace in the nations.

If there is to be peace in the nations,
There must be peace in the cities.

If there is to be peace in the cities,
There must be peace between neighbors.

If there is to be peace between neighbors,
There must be peace in the home.

If there is to be peace in the home,
There must be peace in the heart.

—Lao Tse

The Heart Is Wide

The world stands out on either side
No wider than the heart is wide;
Above the world is stretched the sky,
No higher than the soul is high.
The heart can push the sea and land
Farther away on either hand;
The soul can split the sky in two,
And let the face of God shine through.
But East and West will pinch the heart
That cannot keep them pushed apart;
And he whose soul is flat—the sky
Will cave in on him by and by.

—*Edna St. Vincent Millay*

Fill the Day with Love

Start the Day with Love;
Spend the Day with Love;
Fill the Day with Love;
End the Day with Love;
This is the way to God.

—*Sri Sathya Sai Baba*

Open the Window to Love

There is some kiss we want
with our whole lives,
the touch of Spirit on the body.
Seawater begs the pearl
to break its shell.
And the lily, how passionately
it needs some wild Darling!
At night, I open the window
and ask the moon to come
and press its face into mine.
Breathe into me.
Close the language-door,
and open the love-window.
The moon won't use the door,
only the window.

—*Jalal al-Din Rumi, thirteenth century Persian poet*

Songs of the Heart

At the still point of the universe
all that is not silence is song.
And all creation, hearing it, dances for joy.
The song of the universe is the song of life,
its rhythms defined by the cadence of time,
its beauty in its holy harmony.
The song is sung best when sung by the heart.

—*Alfred V. Fedak*

Make a Little Music with Your Heart

When the song of the angels is stilled,
when the star in the sky is gone,
when the kings and princes are home,
when the shepherds are back with the flocks,
then the work of Christmas begins:
To find the lost, to heal those broken in spirit,
to feed the hungry, to release the oppressed,
to rebuild the nations, to bring peace among all peoples,
to make a little music with the heart.
And to radiate the Light of Christ, every day,
in every way, in all that we do and in all that we say.
Then the work of Christmas begins.

—Howard Thurman

Acts of Love

This new Bible shall be written
On the hearts of all mankind,
Not by pen or book,
But by acts of Love.
For to Love as She does
Is to truly know who He is.
The unchanged truth is eternal life
For all, without exception.
For no longer do we wander lost in the Word,
But live the word in eternal life.

—Justina M. Pernetter

Love

And I saw the river
over which every soul must pass
to reach the kingdom of heaven
and the name of that river was suffering—
and I saw the boat
which carries souls across the river
and the name of that boat was
love.

—*Saint John of the Cross*

Prayer

Prayer is a surge of the heart, it is a simple look
turned toward heaven, it is a cry of recognition and of love,
embracing both trial and joy.

—*St. Therese of Lisieux*

Your Love

Bless us with Love, O Merciful God;
That we may Love as you Love!
That we may show patience, tolerance,
Kindness, caring and love to all!
Give me knowledge; O giver of Knowledge,
That I may be one with my Universe and Mother Earth!
O Compassionate One, grant compassion unto us;
That we may help all fellow souls in need!
Bless us with your Love O God.
Bless us with your Love.

—*Author Unknown*

Give All to Love

Give all to love;
Obey thy heart;
Friends, kindred, days,
Estate, good-fame,
Plans, credit and the Muse—
Nothing refuse.

'Tis a brave master;
Let it have scope:
Follow it utterly,
Hope beyond hope:
High and more high
It dives into noon,
With wing unspent,
Untold intent;

But it is a god,
Knows its own path
And the outlets of the sky.

It was never for the mean;
It requireth courage stout.
Souls above doubt,
Valor unbending,
It will reward,
—They shall return
More than they were,
And ever ascending.

Leave all for love;
Yet, hear me, yet,
One word more thy heart behoved,
One pulse more of firm endeavor,
—Keep thee today,
Tomorrow, forever,
Free as an Arab
Of thy beloved.

Cling with life to the maid;
But when the surprise,
First vague shadow of surmise
Flits across her bosom young,
Of a joy apart from thee,
Free be she, fancy-free;
Nor thou detain her vesture's hem,
Nor the palest rose she flung
From her summer diadem.

Though thou loved her as thyself,
As a self of purer clay,
Though her parting dims the day,
Stealing grace from all alive;
Heartily know,
When half-gods go.
The gods arrive.

—*Ralph Waldo Emerson*

It's All I Have to Bring Today

It's all I have to bring today—
This, and my heart beside—
This, and my heart, and all the fields—
And all the meadows wide—
Be sure you count—should I forget
Some one the sum could tell—
This, and my heart, and all the Bees
Which in the Clover dwell.

—*Emily Dickinson*

Friendship

A ruddy drop of manly blood
The surging sea outweighs,
The world uncertain comes and goes;
The lover rooted stays.
I fancied he was fled—
And, after many a year,
Glowed unexhausted kindliness,
Like daily sunrise there.
My careful heart was free again,
O friend, my bosom said,
Through thee alone the sky is arched,
Through thee the rose is red;
All things through thee take nobler form,
And look beyond the earth,
The mill-round of our fate appears
A sun-path in thy worth.
Me too thy nobleness has taught
To master my despair;
The fountains of my hidden life
Are through thy friendship fair.

—*Ralph Waldo Emerson*

Love, Time, and Will

A soul immortal, Time, God everywhere,
Without, within—how can a heart despair,
Or talk of failure, obstacles, and doubt?
(What proofs of God? The little seeds that sprout,
Life, and the solar system, and their laws.
Nature? Ah, yes; but what was Nature's cause?)

All mighty words are short: God, life, and death,
War, peace, and truth are uttered in a breath.
And briefly said are love, and will, and time;
Yet in them lies a majesty sublime.

Love is the vast constructive power of space;
Time is the hour which calls it into place;
Will is the means of using time and love,
And bringing forth the heart's desires thereof.

The way is love, the time is now, and will
The patient method. Let this knowledge fill
Thy consciousness, and fate and circumstance,
Environment, and all the ills of chance
Must yield before the concentrated might
Of those three words, as shadows yield to light.

Go, charge thyself with love; be infinite
And opulent with thy large use of it:
'Tis from free sowing that full harvest springs;
Love God and life and all created things.

Learn time's great value; to this mandate bow,
The hour of opportunity is Now,
And from thy will, as from a well-strung bow,

Let the swift arrows of thy wishes go.
Though sent into the distance and the dark,
The dawn shall prove thy arrows hit the mark.

—Ella Wheeler Wilcox

There Is Light Somewhere

Your life is your life
don't let it be clubbed into dank submission.
be on the watch.
there are ways out.
there is light somewhere.
it may not be much light but
            it beats the darkness.

—Charles Bukowski (1885)

Lay Not Up for Yourselves

Lay not up for yourselves

treasures upon the earth,
where moth and rust doth corrupt,
and where thieves break though and steal:

But lay up for yourselves

treasures in heaven,
where neither moth nor rust doth corrupt,
and where thieves do not break through nor steal:

For where your treasure is,
there will your heart be also.

—St. Matthew, 6:19–21 (King James version)

Felt with the Heart

The best and most beautiful things in the world cannot
be seen or even touched—they must be
felt with the heart.

—Helen Keller

Precious Friend

How can I find the shining word, the glowing phrase
that tells all that your love has meant to me, all that
your friendship spells? There is no word, no phrase for
you on whom I so depend. All I can say to you is this,
God bless you, precious friend.

—Grace Noll Crowell

Love's Philosophy

The fountains mingle with the river
And the rivers with the ocean,
The winds of heaven mix for ever
With a sweet emotion;
Nothing in the world is single;
All things by a law divine
In one spirit meet and mingle.
Why not I with thine?

See the mountains kiss high heaven
And the waves clasp one another;
No sister-flower would be forgiven
If it disdained its brother;
And the sunlight clasps the earth
And the moonbeams kiss the sea:
What is all this sweet work worth
If thou kiss not me?

—*Percy Bysshe Shelley*

A Song

Life is but a troubled ocean,
Hope a meteor, love a flower
Which blossoms in the morning beam,
And withers with the evening hour.

Ambition is a dizzy height,
And glory, but a lightning gleam;
Fame is a bubble, dazzling bright,
Which fairest shines in fortune's beam.

When clouds and darkness veil the skies,
And sorrow's blast blows loud and chill,
Friendship shall like a rainbow rise,
And softly whisper—peace, be still.

—*Lucretia Maria Davidson*

A Friend's Greeting

I'd like to be the sort of friend
that you have been to me;
I'd like to be the help that you've been
always glad to be;
I'd like to mean as much to you
each minute of the day
As you have meant, old friend of mine,
to me along the way.

I'd like to do the big things
and the splendid things for you,
To brush the gray out of your skies
and leave them only blue;
I'd like to say the kindly things
that I so oft have heard,
And feel that I could rouse your soul
the way that mine you've stirred.

I'd like to give back the joy
that you have given me,
Yet that were wishing you a need
I hope will never be;
I'd like to make you feel
as rich as I, who travel on
Undaunted in the darkest hours
with you to lean upon.

I'm wishing at this Christmas time
that I could but repay
A portion of the gladness
that you've strewn along the way;
And could I have one wish this year,
this only would it be:
I'd like to be the sort of friend
that you have been to me.

—*Edgar Guest*

Friends

How good to lie a little while
And look up through the tree!
The Sky is like a kind big smile
Bent sweetly over me.

The Sunshine flickers through the lace
Of leaves above my head,
And kisses me upon the face
Like Mother, before bed.

The Wind comes stealing o'er the grass
To whisper pretty things;
And though I cannot see him pass,
I feel his careful wings.

So many gentle Friends are near
Whom one can scarcely see,
A child should never feel a fear,
Wherever he may be.

—*Abbie Farwell Brown*

The Gift of a Friend

A friend is a gift you give yourself.

—*Betsy Patterson, 1917*

March

Winds of Change

"One day at a time, one step at a time, and you'll get there."

—BILL W.

"Figure out how to climb it, go through it, or work around it."

—MICHAEL JORDAN

"What is coming is better than what has gone."

—JANICE JOHNS

"The trick is to enjoy life. Don't wish away your days, waiting for better ones ahead."

—MARJORIE PAY HINCKLEY

"It is never too late to be what you might have been."

—GEORGE ELIOT (NÉE MARY ANN EVANS)

"Everyone thinks of changing the world, but no one thinks of changing himself."

—LEO TOLSTOY

God's Time Is Always Near

"God's time is always near.
He set the North Star in the heavens;
He gave me the strength in my limbs;
He meant I should be free."

—*Harriet Tubman, circa 1859*

Lead Us to Light and Truth

Asatho Maa Sad Gamaya.
Thamaso Maa Jyothir Gamaya.
Mrithyur Maa Amritham Gamaya.
Om Shanti, Shanti, Shanti.
From untruth, lead us to Truth.
From darkness, lead us to Light.
From death. lead us to Immortality.
Om Peace, Peace, Peace.

—*Ancient Vedic Prayer*

A Light Exists in Spring

A light exists in spring
Not present on the year
At any other period.
When March is scarcely here

A color stands abroad
On solitary hills
That science cannot overtake,
But human nature feels.

It waits upon the lawn;
It shows the furthest tree
Upon the furthest slope we know;
It almost speaks to me.

Then, as horizons step,
Or noons report away,
Without the formula of sound,
It passes, and we stay:

A quality of loss
Affecting our content,
As trade had suddenly encroached
Upon a sacrament.

—Emily Dickinson

Give Me Strength for Today and Hope for Tomorrow

God, hear my prayer,
And let my cry come to You.
Do not hide from me in the day of my distress;
Turn to me and speedily answer my prayer.
Eternal God, Source of healing,
Out of my distress I call upon You.
Help me sense Your presence
At this difficult time.
Grant me patience when the hours are heavy;
In hurt or disappointment, give me courage.
Keep me trustful in Your love.
Give me strength for today, and hope for tomorrow.
To your loving hands I commit my spirit
When asleep and when awake. You are with me;
I shall not fear.

—*Traditional Jewish Healing Prayer*

Take Positive Action

In a time of destruction, create something.
A poem.
A parade.
A community.
A school.
A vow.
A moral principle.
One peaceful moment.

—Maxine Hong Kingston

Happiness Is Worth Striving For

You are a child of the universe,
no less than the trees and the stars;
you have a right to be here.
And whether or not it is clear to you,
no doubt the universe is unfolding as it should.

Therefore be at peace with God,
whatever you conceive Him to be,
and whatever your labors and aspirations,
in the noisy confusion of life keep peace with your soul.
With all its sham, drudgery, and broken dreams,
it is still a beautiful world.
Be cheerful.
Strive to be happy.

—Max Ehrmann, 1927

Try Looking at Things a Different Way

Mindfulness: taking a balanced approach to negative
emotions so that feelings are neither suppressed nor
exaggerated. We cannot ignore our pain and feel compassion
for it at the same time. Mindfulness requires that we
not "over-identify" with thoughts and feelings so that
we are caught up and swept away by negativity.

—Brené Brown

Keep Looking for the Open Doors

When one door of happiness closes,
another opens,
but often we look so long
at the closed door
that we do not see the one
that has been opened for us.

—Helen Keller

The Courage to Serve Others

Show me the suffering of the most miserable;
So I will know my people's plight.

Free me to pray for others;
For you are present in every person.

Help me take responsibility for my own life;
So that I can be free at last.

Grant me courage to serve others;
For in service there is true life.

Give me honesty and patience;
So that the Spirit will be alive among us.

Let the Spirit flourish and grow;
So that we will never tire of the struggle.

Let us remember those who have died for justice;
For they have given us life.

Help us love even those who hate us;
So we can change the world.

Amen.

—César E. Chávez, American civil rights activist

Look Upon Us

Look upon us, O Lord,
and let all the darkness of our souls
vanish before the beams of thy brightness.
Fill us with holy love,
and open to us the treasures of thy wisdom.
All our desire is known unto thee,
therefore perfect what thou hast begun,
and what thy Spirit has awakened us to ask in prayer.
We seek thy face,
turn thy face unto us and show us thy glory.
Then shall our longing be satisfied,
and our peace shall be perfect.

—*St. Augustine*

Gaelic Blessing

May the road rise up to meet you.
May the wind be always at your back.
May the sun shine warm upon your face;
the rains fall soft upon your fields, and until we meet again,
may God hold you in the palm of His hand.

—*Traditional Gaelic Blessing*

To Everything There Is a Season

To everything there is a season,
a time for every purpose under the sun.
A time to be born and a time to die;
a time to plant and a time to pluck up that which is planted;
a time to kill and a time to heal…
a time to weep and a time to laugh;
a time to mourn and a time to dance…
a time to embrace and a time to refrain from embracing;
a time to lose and a time to seek;
a time to rend and a time to sew;
a time to keep silent and a time to speak;
a time to love and a time to hate;
a time for war and a time for peace.

—Ecclesiastes 3:1–8

Life's Privilege

When you arise in the
morning, think of what a precious
privilege it is to be alive—to
breathe, to think, to enjoy, to love.

—Marcus Aurelius

I Arise Today

I arise today through God's strength to pilot me:
God's might to uphold me,
God's wisdom to guide me,
God's eye to look before me,
God's ear to hear me,
God's word to speak for me,
God's hand to guard me,
God's way to lie before me,
God's shield to protect me,
God's host to secure me:
against snares of devils,
against temptations of vices,
against inclinations of nature,
against everyone who shall wish me ill,
afar and anear, alone and in a crowd.

—Breastplate of St. Patrick—433 CE

Past and Future

My future will not copy fair my past
On any leaf but Heaven's. Be fully done,
Supernal Will! I would not fain be one
Who, satisfying thirst and breaking fast
Upon the fulness of the heart, at last
Saith no grace after meat. My wine hath run
Indeed out of my cup, and there is none

To gather up the bread of my repast
Scattered and trampled! Yet I find some good
In earth's green herbs, and streams that bubble up
Clear from the darkling ground, content until
I sit with angels before better food.
Dear Christ! when thy new vintage fills my cup,
This hand shall shake no more, nor that wine spill.

—*Elizabeth Barrett Browning*

When Traveling Is Hard

When traveling is hard;
mountains to climb,
rivers to cross,
storms that assail,
and in our own strength
we know that we shall fail,
Lord, reach out your hand
to guide us safely,
and without stumbling,
toward our journey's end.

—*Anonymous*

Help Us Live Today

O God, we thank you for the gift of this day.
Give us the energy we need to face our work,
with the attentiveness we need to do it well.
Give us the self-discipline we need to finish it
even if no one sees and no one praises us.
Give us the self-respect which will inspire us
not to produce anything which is less than our best.
Give us the courtesy and the considerateness
which will make us easy to live and work with.
Help us to live today so that we will make the world
a happier more hopeful place wherever we go.
Amen!

—*William Barclay*

Everyone Sang

Everyone suddenly burst out singing;
And I was filled with such delight
As prisoned birds must find in freedom
Winging wildly across the white
Orchards and dark green fields; on; on; and out of sight.

Everyone's voice was suddenly lifted,
And beauty came like the setting sun.
My heart was shaken with tears and horror
Drifted away… O but every one
Was a bird; and the song was wordless; the singing will
never be done.

—*Siegfried Sassoon*

I Have a Rendezvous with Life

I have a rendezvous with Life,
In days I hope will come,
Ere youth has sped, and strength of mind,
Ere voices sweet grow dumb.
I have a rendezvous with Life,
When Spring's first heralds hum.
Sure some would cry it's better far
To crown their days with sleep
Than face the road, the wind and rain,
To heed the calling deep.
Though wet nor blow nor space I fear,
Yet fear I deeply, too,
Lest Death should meet and claim me ere
I keep Life's rendezvous.

—*Countee Cullen*

Quest

My goal out-distances the utmost star,
Yet is encompassed in my inmost Soul;
I am my goal—my quest, to know myself.
To chart and compass this unfathomed sea,
Myself must plumb the boundless universe.
My Soul contains all thought, all mystery,
All wisdom of the Great Infinite Mind:
This is to discover, I must voyage far,
At last to find it in my pulsing heart.

—*Carrie Williams Clifford*

The World's Wanderers

Tell me, thou star, whose wings of light
Speed thee in thy fiery flight,
In what cavern of the night
Will thy pinions close now?

Tell me, moon, thou pale and grey
Pilgrim of heaven's homeless way,
In what depth of night or day
Seekest thou repose now?

Weary wind, who wanderest
Like the world's rejected guest,
Hast thou still some secret nest
On the tree or billow?

—*Percy Bysshe Shelley*

For Strength and Guidance

Lord God Almighty,
shaper and ruler of all creatures,
we pray for your great mercy,
that you guide us toward you,
for we cannot find our way.
And guide us to your will, to the need of our soul,
for we cannot do it ourselves.
And make our mind steadfast in your will
and aware of our soul's need.
Strengthen us against the temptations of the devil,
and remove from us all lust and every unrighteousness,
and shield us against our foes, seen and unseen.

Teach us to do your will,
that we may inwardly love you before
all things with a pure mind.
For you are our maker and our redeemer,
our help, our comfort, our trust, our hope;
praise and glory be to you now and forever.

—*Alfred the Great, ninth century*

Song of the Open Road

Allons! whoever you are come travel with me!
Traveling with me you find what never tires.

The earth never tires,
The earth is rude, silent, incomprehensible at first,
Nature is rude and incomprehensible at first,
Be not discouraged, keep on, there are
divine things well envelop'd,
I swear to you there are divine things more
beautiful than words can tell.

Allons! we must not stop here,
However sweet these laid-up stores,
however convenient this dwelling we cannot remain here,
However shelter'd this port
and however calm these waters we must not anchor here,
However welcome the hospitality that surrounds us
we are permitted to receive it but a little while.

—*Walt Whitman*

The Bravest of Us

The bravest are surely those who have the clearest
vision of what is before them, glory and danger alike,
and yet notwithstanding, go out to meet it.

—*Thucydides*

Why I Smile

I smile because the world is fair;
Because the sky is blue.
Because I find, no matter where
I go, a friend that's true.

I smile because the earth is green,
The sun so near and bright,
Because the days that o'er us lean
Are full of warmth and light.

I smile as past the yards I go,
Though strange and new the place,
The violets seem my step to know,
And look up in my face.

I smile to hear the robin's note.
He comes so newly dressed,
A love song throbbing in his throat,
A rose pinned on his breast.

And so the truth I'll not disown:
Because the spring is nigh,
My heart has somewhat better grown,
And I forget to sigh.

—*Kate Slaughter McKinney*

Small Beginnings

A traveler on the dusty road
Strewed acorns on the lea;
And one took root and sprouted up,
And grew into a tree.
Love sought its shade, at evening time,
To breathe his early vows;
And age was pleased, in heats of noon,
To bask beneath its boughs;
The dormouse loved its dangling twigs,
The birds sweet music bore;
It stood a glory in its place,
A blessing evermore.

—*Charles Mackay*

Now Is the Time to Understand More

Nothing in life is to be feared,
it is only to be understood.
Now is the time to understand more,
so that we may fear less.

—*Marie Curie*

Moving Forward Together

Every moment wasted looking back
keeps us from moving forward.
In this world and the world of tomorrow,
we must go forward together or not at all.

—Hillary Clinton

Unconditional Love

The unconditional love we experience
will rejuvenate our will to live,
and each positive move on our part will
be matched by an unexpected opportunity.

—Narcotics Anonymous

All Things Have Become New

Therefore, if anyone is in Christ, he is a new creation;
old things have passed away; behold,
all things have become new.

—2 Corinthians 5:17

The Further We Travel

Life is an unfoldment, and the further we travel,
the more truth we can comprehend.

—Hypatia of Alexandria

April

Springing into Action

"There are secrets opportunities hidden inside every failure."

—SOPHIA AMORUSO

"Great works are performed not by
strength but by perseverance."

—SAMUEL JOHNSON

"The energy of the mind is the essence of life."

—ARISTOTLE

"Strength does not come from physical capacity.
It comes from an indomitable will."

—MAHATMA GANDHI

"Action is the foundational key to all success."

—PABLO PICASSO

Prayer for the Right Path

Doing the right thing is our best gift
That is what brings us bliss and happiness
Happy and blissful is the person who does what is right,
because it is the right thing to do

—*Ancient Zoroastrian Chant*

Chant for the Sacred Earth

Cover my earth mother four times with many flowers.
Let the heavens be covered with the banked-up clouds.
Let the earth be covered with fog;
cover the earth with rains.
Great waters, rains, cover the earth.
Lightning cover the earth.
Let thunder be heard over the earth;
let thunder be heard;
Let thunder be heard over the six regions of the earth.

—*Native American Oral Tradition*

Live As If Today Is Your Last

Ah, Fill the cup—

What boots it to repeat
How time is slipping underneath our feet,
Unborn Tomorrow,
And dead Yesterday
Why fret about them

If Today be sweet!!

—*Omar Khayyam*

Bloom Where You Are Planted

I am, O my God,
but a tiny seed which Thou hast sown
in the soil of Thy love
and caused to spring forth by the hand of Thy bounty.
This seed craveth, therefore,
in its inmost being,
the waters of Thy mercy
and the living fountain of Thy grace.
Send down upon it
from the heaven of Thy loving-kindness
that which will enable it to flourish beneath Thy shadow
and within the borders of Thy court.
Thou art He Who watereth the hearts of all
that have recognized Thee from Thy plenteous stream
and the fountain of Thy living waters.
Praised be to God,
the Lord of the worlds.

—*Medieval Chant*

Being Thankful for Each New Challenge

Be thankful that you don't already have everything you desire;
If you did, what would there be to look forward to?

Be thankful when you don't know something,
For it gives you the opportunity to learn.

Be thankful for the difficult times.
During those times you grow.

Be thankful for your limitations
Because they give you opportunities for improvement.

Be thankful for each new challenge
Because it will build your strength and character.

Be thankful for your mistakes
They will teach you valuable lessons.

Be thankful when you're tired and weary
Because it means you've made a difference.

It is easy to be thankful for the good things.
A life of rich fulfillment comes to those who are
also thankful for the setbacks.

Gratitude can turn a negative into a positive.

Find a way to be thankful for your troubles
and they can become your blessing.

—*Anonymous*

One Flower

One flower
on the cliffside
Nodding at the canyon.

—*Jack Kerouac*

Awaken into Your Story

May a good vision catch me
May a benevolent vision take hold of me, and move me
May a deep and full vision come over
me, and burst open around me
May a luminous vision inform me, enfold me.
May I awaken into the story that surrounds,
May I awaken into the beautiful story.
May the wondrous story find me;
May the wildness that makes beauty arise between two lovers
arise beautifully between my body and the body of this land,
between my flesh and the flesh of this earth,
here and now,
on this day,
May I taste something sacred.

—*David Abram*

Feel the Fear and Do It Anyway

I learned that courage
was not the absence of fear,
but the triumph over it.
The brave man is not he
who does not feel afraid,
but he who conquers that fear.

—*Nelson Mandela*

Spring Morning

O day—if I could cup my hands and drink of you,
And make this shining wonder be
A part of me!
O day! O day!
You lift and sway your colors on the sky
Till I am crushed with beauty. Why is there
More of reeling sunlit air
Than I can breathe? Why is there sound
In silence? Why is a singing wound
About each hour?
And perfume when there is no flower?
O day! O Day! How may I press
Nearer to loveliness?

—*Marion Strubel*

When I Rise Up

When I rise up above the earth,
And look down on the things that fetter me,
I beat my wings upon the air,
Or tranquil lie,
Surge after surge of potent strength
Like incense comes to me
When I rise up above the earth
And look down upon the things that fetter me.

—*Georgia Douglas Johnson*

Tomorrow

Get up tomorrow early in the morning, and earlier than you did today, and do the best that you can. Always stay near me, for tomorrow I will have much to do and more than I ever had, and tomorrow blood will leave my body above the breast.

—*Joan of Arc*

Great Spirit Prayer

Oh, Great Spirit,
Whose voice I hear in the winds
and whose breath gives life to all the world.
Hear me! I need your strength and wisdom.
Let me walk in beauty, and make my eyes
ever hold the red and purple sunset.
Make my hands respect the things you have made
and my ears sharp to hear your voice.
Make me wise so that I may understand
the things you have taught my people.
Let me learn the lessons you have hidden
in every leaf and rock.

Help me remain calm and strong in the
face of all that comes toward me.
Help me find compassion without
empathy overwhelming me.
I seek strength, not to be greater than my brother,
but to fight my greatest enemy: myself.
Make me always ready to come to you
with clean hands and straight eyes.
So when life fades as the fading sunset,
my spirit may come to you without shame.

—Translated by Lakota Sioux Chief Yellow Lark in 1887

Your Loving Support

God, oh God, it is you I seek.
And with your constant loving support
I will even try to seek you in lost causes,
those dark and forgotten places that
I can't imagine you present.
And yet you are there.
Help me to be there too,
seeking, finding, proclaiming your goodness
even as the day darkens
and my spirit draws back to my false safety of self.
Fill me with wonder of your goodness,
replacing my self-doubt with confidence
in you and your sure and steady help.

—*Author Unknown*

A Psalm of Life

Tell me not, in mournful numbers,
Life is but an empty dream!
For the soul is dead that slumbers,
And things are not what they seem.

Life is real! Life is earnest!
And the grave is not its goal;
Dust thou art, to dust returnest,
Was not spoken of the soul.

Not enjoyment, and not sorrow,
Is our destined end or way;
But to act, that each tomorrow
Find us farther than today.

Art is long, and Time is fleeting,
And our hearts, though stout and brave,
Still, like muffled drums, are beating
Funeral marches to the grave.

In the world's broad field of battle,
In the bivouac of Life,
Be not like dumb, driven cattle!
Be a hero in the strife!

Trust no Future, howe'er pleasant!
Let the dead Past bury its dead!
Act—act in the living Present!
Heart within, and God o'erhead!

Lives of great men all remind us
We can make our lives sublime,
And, departing, leave behind us
Footprints on the sands of time;

Footprints, that perhaps another,
Sailing o'er life's solemn main,
A forlorn and shipwrecked brother,
Seeing, shall take heart again.

Let us, then, be up and doing,
With a heart for any fate;
Still achieving, still pursuing,
Learn to labor and to wait.

—*Henry Wadsworth Longfellow*

The Human Seasons

Four Seasons fill the measure of the year;
There are four seasons in the mind of man:
He has his lusty Spring, when fancy clear
Takes in all beauty with an easy span:
He has his Summer, when luxuriously
Spring's honied cud of youthful thought he loves
To ruminate, and by such dreaming high
Is nearest unto heaven: quiet coves
His soul has in its Autumn, when his wings
He furleth close; contented so to look
On mists in idleness, to let fair things
Pass by unheeded as a threshold brook.
He has his Winter too of pale misfeature,
Or else he would forego his mortal nature.

—*John Keats*

Spring Song

A blue-bell springs upon the ledge,
A lark sits singing in the hedge;
Sweet perfumes scent the balmy air,
And life is brimming everywhere.
What lark and breeze and bluebird sing,
Is Spring, Spring, Spring!

No more the air is sharp and cold;
The planter wends across the wold,
And glad beneath the shining sky
We wander forth, my love and I.
And ever in our hearts doth ring
This song of Spring, Spring!

For life is life and love is love,
'Twixt maid and man or dove and dove.
Life may be short, life may be long,
But love will come, and to its song
Shall this refrain for ever cling
Of Spring, Spring, Spring!

—*Paul Laurence Dunbar*

Help Me to Not Be Negative

I am one with my father and the universe.

I am one with mother earth.

I am one with everyone within the reach of my voice.
And, in this togetherness, we ask the divine
intelligence toeradicate all
negatives from our hearts, from our minds,
from our words, and from our actions.

And so be it.

—*Babatunde Olatunji*

A Wintry Sonnet

A robin said: The Spring will never come,
And I shall never care to build again.
A Rosebush said: These frosts are wearisome,
My sap will never stir for sun or rain.
The half Moon said: These nights are fogged and slow,
I neither care to wax nor care to wane.
The Ocean said: I thirst from long ago,
Because earth's rivers cannot fill the main.
When springtime came, red Robin built a nest,
And trilled a lover's song in sheer delight.
Gray hoarfrost vanished, and the Rose with might
Clothed her in leaves and buds of crimson core.
The dim Moon brightened. Ocean sunned his crest,
Dimpled his blue, —yet thirsted evermore.

—*Christina Georgina Rossetti*

When I used to focus on the worries, everybody
        was ahead of me, I was the bottom
        of the totem pole,
        a largely spread squat animal.

How about a quick massage now, he said to me.
I don't think it's cool, I replied.
Oh, said he, after a pause, I should have waited
        for *you* to ask *me*.

The waves came in closer and closer.

When I fall into the gap of suspicion I am no
        longer here.

In this world that has got closed over by houses
        and networks, I fly out
from under the belly. Life's dizzy crown
of whirling lights, circles this head. Pure
with wonder, hot
with wonder. The streets become golden. All
size increases, the colors glow, we are in myth.

—*Joanne Kyger*

A Thing of Beauty

A thing of beauty is a joy for ever:
Its loveliness increases; it will never
Pass into nothingness; but still will keep
A bower quiet for us, and a sleep
Full of sweet dreams, and health, and quiet breathing.
Therefore, on every morrow, are we wreathing
A flowery band to bind us to the earth,
Spite of despondence, of the inhuman dearth
Of noble natures, of the gloomy days,
Of all the unhealthy and o'er-dark'n'd ways
Made for our searching: yes, in spite of all,
Some shape of beauty moves away the pall
From our dark spirits. Such the sun, the moon,
Trees old and young, sprouting a shady boon
For simple sheep; and such are daffodils
With the green world they live in; and clear rills
That for themselves a cooling covert make
'Gainst the hot season; the mid-forest brake,
Rich with a sprinkling of fair musk-rose blooms:
And such too is the grandeur of the dooms
We have imagined for the mighty dead;
An endless fountain of immortal drink,
Pouring unto us from the heaven's brink.

—*John Keats*

Inspire Me to Kindness, Each and Every Day

Day by day,
Let me see the grace
Day by day,
Let me see the way

Day by day,
Let me see the beauty
Let me hear the music
Day by day
Let me see the way

Day by day
Let me see the goodness
Let me feel the love
Inspire me to kindness
Day by day,
Let me see the way

Let me see the grace

Let me see the way

—Hans van Rostenberghe

The Hope of Spring

God, thank you for spring and the hope of warmer,
longer, brighter days.
Thank you for the coming of growth and life and birth.
Thank you that things are coming awake in the world.
This is what our calendar says, and we do see
some signs that it is real.
But we also still struggle with the residual layover of winter.
Now we ask that you bring into reality all
that belongs in this season.
Your word says that we will have provision, and hope, and joy,
and health and loving relationships here and now in this life.
We ask that what belongs in this season would
become actual in our practical lives.
We hope in you and in your promises. We hope
in your gift of spring.

—*Author Unknown*

Bless Our Feet

Bless our feet
that they might tread
the path prepared.
Bless our hands
that they might show
your love's embrace.
Bless our words
that they might share
your grace and peace.

—*Celtic Prayer*

Spring, the Sweet Spring

Spring, the sweet spring, is the year's pleasant king,
Then blooms each thing, then maids dance in a ring,
Cold doth not sting, the pretty birds do sing:
Cuckoo, jug-jug, pu-we, to-witta-woo!

The palm and may make country houses gay,
Lambs frisk and play, the shepherds pipe all day,
And we hear aye birds tune this merry lay:
Cuckoo, jug-jug, pu-we, to-witta-woo!

The fields breathe sweet, the daisies kiss our feet,
Young lovers meet, old wives a-sunning sit,
In every street these tunes our ears do greet:
Cuckoo, jug-jug, pu-we, to-witta-woo!
Spring, the sweet spring!

—*Thomas Nashe*

Sonnet

I had no thought of violets of late,
The wild, shy kind that spring beneath your feet
In wistful April days, when lovers mate
And wander through the fields in raptures sweet.
The thought of violets meant florists' shops,
And bows and pins, and perfumed papers fine;
And garish lights, and mincing little fops
And cabarets and songs, and deadening wine.
So far from sweet real things my thoughts had strayed,
I had forgot wide fields, and clear brown streams;
The perfect loveliness that God has made—

Wild violets shy and Heaven-mounting dreams.
And now—unwittingly, you've made me dream
Of violets, and my soul's forgotten gleam.

—*Alice Dunbar-Nelson*

A Spring Morning

The Spring comes in with all her hues and smells,
In freshness breathing over hills and dells;
O'er woods where May her gorgeous drapery flings,
And meads washed fragrant by their laughing springs.
Fresh are new-opened flowers, untouched and free
From the bold rifling of the amorous bee.
The happy time of singing birds is come,
And Love's lone pilgrimage now finds a home;
Among the mossy oaks now coos the dove,
And the hoarse crow finds softer notes for love.
The foxes play around their dens, and bark
In joy's excess, 'mid woodland shadows dark.
The flowers join lips below; the leaves above;
And every sound that meets the ear is Love.

—*John Clare*

Windflower

The wind stooped down and wrote a sweet, small word,
But the snow fell, and all the writing blurred:
Now, the snow gone, we read it as we pass—
The wind's word in the grass.

—Lizette Woodworth Reese

Just One Step

Do the difficult things while they are easy
and do the great things while they are small.
A journey of a thousand miles must begin with a single step.

—Lao Tse

The Lord Is My Portion

The steadfast love of the Lord never ceases;
His mercies never come to an end;
They are new every morning; great is your faithfulness.
"The Lord is my portion," says my soul,
"therefore I will hope in him."

—Lamentations 3:22–24

Music

Sweet melody amidst the moving spheres
Breaks forth, a solemn and entrancing sound,
A harmony whereof the earth's green hills
Give but the faintest echo; yet is there
A music everywhere, and concert sweet!
All birds which sing amidst the forest deep
Till the flowers listen with unfolded bells;
All winds that murmur over summer grass,
Or curl the waves upon the pebbly shore;
Chiefly all earnest human voices rais'd
In charity and for the cause of truth,
Mingle together in one sacred chord,
And float, a grateful incense, up to God.

—Bessie Rayner Parkes

May

Kindnesses Abound

"When we give cheerfully and accept
gratefully, everyone is blessed."

—MAYA ANGELOU

"Life isn't about getting and having,
it's about giving and being."

—KEVIN KRUSE

"We can't help everyone, but everyone can help someone."

—RONALD REAGAN

"Walking with a friend in the dark is better
than walking alone in the light."

—HELEN KELLER

"Sometimes it takes only one act of
kindness to change a person's life."

—JACKIE CHAN

"Kindness is like snow—it beautifies everything it covers."

—KAHLIL GIBRAN

Now spring appears, with beauty crowned
And all is light and life around,
Why comes not Jane? When friendship calls,
Why leaves she not Augusta's walls?
Where cooling zephyrs faintly blow,
Nor spread the cheering, healthful glow
That glides through each awakened vein,
As skimming o'er the spacious plain,
We look around with joyous eye,
And view no boundaries but the sky.

Already April's reign is o'er,
Her evening tints delight no more;
No more the violet scents the gale,
No more the mist o'erspreads the vale;
The lovely queen of smiles and tears,
Who gave thee birth, no more appears;
But blushing May, with brow serene,
And vestments of a livelier green,
Commands the winged choir to sing,
And with wild notes the meadows ring.

O come! ere all the train is gone,
No more to hail thy twenty-one;
That age which higher honour shares,
And well become the wreath it wears.
From lassitude and cities flee,
And breathe the air of heaven with me.

—*Matilda Bethem*

My Religion Is Kindness

If you wish to experience peace, provide peace for another.
If you wish to know that you are safe, cause another to know
that they are safe.
If you wish to better understand seemingly
incomprehensible things,
help another to better understand.
If you wish to heal your own sadness or anger, seek to heal the
sadness or anger of another.
Those others are waiting for you now. They are looking to you
for guidance,
for help, for courage, for strength, for understanding, and for
assurance at this hour.
Most of all, they are looking to you for love.
My religion is very simple.
My religion is kindness.

—*His Holiness the fourteenth Dalai Lama, 1981*

Practice Random Acts of Kindness

Be kind,
for everyone
you meet
is fighting
a hard
battle.

—*adaptation of John Watson, writing as Ian MacLaren, 1898*

Emergence

At the depths of despair, nothing matters,
I can't do anything, got to get out of here,
walls falling in, throw me a rope, I can't move,
can't stand it, nothing, throw me a rope…

And one day, like any other day, finally tired of
waiting for help
that never comes, make a rope, tie it to a rock throw it up pull
yourself out and walk away…

And it took all that time
just to find yourself.

And that's how long it had to take;
and it was well worth every moment.

—*Paul Williams*

Thy Neighbor as Thyself

Let the warmth of the sun heal us
wherever we are broken.
Let it burn away the fog so that
we can see each other clearly.
So that we can see beyond labels,
beyond accents, gender or skin color.
Let the warmth and brightness
of the sun melt our selfishness.
So that we can share the joys and
feel the sorrows of our neighbors.
And let the light of the sun
be so strong that we will see all
people as our neighbors.
Let the earth, nourished by rain,
bring forth flowers
to surround us with beauty.
And let the mountains teach our hearts
to reach upward to heaven.

—*Rabbi Harold Kushner*

Make Haste to Be Kind

Life is short and we have not too much time
for gladdening the hearts of those
who are traveling the dark way with us.
Oh, be swift to love! Make haste to be kind.

—*Henri-Frederic Amiel, 1885*

Practice Kindness Day and Night

May we practice kindness day and night,
forever, not only toward friends, but also to
strangers, and especially to the enemy;
not only toward human beings,
but also to animals and other beings
who want happiness and don't want to suffer.

May we constantly enjoy our lives by rejoicing.

May we constantly enjoy happiness
by rejoicing in all the positive things that bring
benefit to others and to ourselves.
And may we especially rejoice when we see
all the good things that happen to others.

May we develop patience to achieve all happiness,
temporal and ultimate, and to bring that
happiness to others; not only to our family,
but to all sentient beings.

May we develop all the sixteen human qualities,
an understanding which makes our lives different.

May we become skilled in not harming sentient beings,
and may we become only the source of happiness
for sentient beings, like sunshine.

May we practice contentment.

May we learn contentment and satisfaction,
an understanding which makes our lives different.

May we learn contentment and satisfaction.
May we learn to enjoy contentment,
which brings great freedom into our lives
and brings us so much happiness.
May we be an example to the world.

May we practice these good qualities
and when somebody abuses or harms us,
may we immediately forgive them.
In daily life, when we make mistakes and harm others,
may we immediately ask forgiveness.

May we be able to develop courage,
to be an inspiring example
and to be of benefit in so many ways for
the happiness of others, not only for ourselves.

—*Lama Zopa Rinpoche*

The Power of Kindness

Kindness in words creates confidence,
Kindness in thinking creates profoundness,
Kindness in giving creates love.

—*Lao Tse*

Reaching Out

O Thou in whose great arms
All the children of earth are embraced,
Here in thy presence we remember
our kinship with all human kind.

We rejoice for those who are in
full health and strength,
Whose ways are ways of pleasantness
and peace.

Our hearts reach out toward those
whose ways are ways of suffering,
of body, mind, or soul.

May it be that thou shalt find us
reaching out to them
Not only with our hearts but with
our hands also,
To help them in the bearing of
their burdens,
To help in the lifting of their
burdens.

—*Robert French Leavens*

First Footsteps

A little way, more soft and sweet
Than fields aflower with May,
A babe's feet, venturing, scarce complete
A little way.

Eyes full of dawning day
Look up for mother's eyes to meet,
Too blithe for song to say.

Glad as the golden spring to greet
Its first live leaflet's play,
Love, laughing, leads the little feet
A little way.

—*Algernon Charles Swinburne*

May Garden

A shower of green gems on my apple tree
This first morning of May
Has fallen out of the night, to be
Herald of holiday—
Bright gems of green that, fallen there,
Seem fixed and glowing on the air.

Until a flutter of blackbird wings
Shakes and makes the boughs alive,
And the gems are now no frozen things,
But apple-green buds to thrive
On sap of my May garden, how well
The green September globes will tell.

Also my pear tree has its buds,
But they are silver-yellow,
Like autumn meadows when the floods
Are silver under willow,
And here shall long and shapely pears
Be gathered while the autumn wears.

And there are sixty daffodils
Beneath my wall...
And jealousy it is that kills
This world when all
The spring's behaviour here is spent
To make the world magnificent

—*John Drinkwater*

May I Be Happy

May I be filled with loving-kindness.
May I be well.
May I be peaceful and at ease.
May I be happy.

—*Ancient Tibetan Meditation*

Begin Again

Finally I saw that worrying had come to nothing.
And gave it up. And took my old body
and went out into the morning,
and sang.

—*Mary Oliver*

Appreciation

Appreciation can change a day, even change a life. Your
willingness to put it into words is all that is necessary.

—*Margaret Cousins*

Inward Peace and Goodwill

O Lord Jesus Christ,
by your incarnation you united
things earthly and heavenly.
Fill us with the sweetness
of inward peace and goodwill,
that we may join the heavenly host
in singing praises to your glory;
for you live and reign
with the Father and the Holy Spirit,
one God, now and forever.
Amen.

—*Georgian Rite, sixth century*

No Kind Action

No kind action ever stops with itself. One kind action
leads to another. Good example is followed. A single act
of kindness throws out roots in all directions, and the
roots spring up and make new trees.
The greatest work that kindness does to others
is that it makes them kind themselves.

—*Amelia Earhart*

The Violet

Down in a green and shady bed,
A modest violet grew,
Its stalk was bent, it hung its head,
As if to hide from view.

And yet it was a lovely flower,
Its colours bright and fair;
It might have graced a rosy bower,
Instead of hiding there,

Yet there it was content to bloom,
In modest tints arrayed;
And there diffused its sweet perfume,
Within the silent shade.

Then let me to the valley go,
This pretty flower to see;
That I may also learn to grow
In sweet humility.

—*Jane Taylor*

Little Things

Little drops of water,
Little grains of sand,
Make the mighty ocean
And the pleasant land.
Little deeds of kindness,
Little words of love,
Make our world an Eden
Like the Heaven above.

—Julia Carney

A Brilliant Day

O keen pellucid air! nothing can lurk
Or disavow itself on this bright day;
The small rain-plashes shine from far away,
The tiny emmet glitters at his work;
The bee looks blithe and gay, and as she plies
Her task, and moves and sidles round the cup
Of this spring flower, to drink its honey up,
Her glassy wings, like oars that dip and rise,
Gleam momently. Pure-bosom'd, clear of fog,
The long lake glistens, while the glorious beam
Bespangles the wet joints and floating leaves
Of water-plants, whose every point receives
His light; and jellies of the spawning frog,
Unmark'd before, like piles of jewels seem!

—Charles Turner

To Live Life

Loving God, help us today;
To live life as an opportunity and benefit from it;
To live life as beauty and admire it;
To live life as a dream and realize it;
To see life as a challenge and meet it;
To live life as duty and complete it;
To see life as a game and play it;
To live life as a promise and fulfill it;
To live life as sorrow and overcome it;
To live life as a song and sing it;
To live life as a struggle and accept it;
To live life as a tragedy and confront it;
To live life as an adventure and dare it;
To live life as luck and make it;
To live life as too precious and not destroy it;
To live life as life and embrace it to the fullest.
Amen!

—*St. Teresa of Calcutta (aka Mother Teresa)*

My People

The night is beautiful,
So the faces of my people.

The stars are beautiful,
So the eyes of my people.

Beautiful, also, is the sun.
Beautiful, also, are the souls of my people.

—*Langston Hughes*

Translation

We trekked into a far country,
My friend and I.
Our deeper content was never spoken,
But each knew all the other said.
He told me how calm his soul was laid
By the lack of anvil and strife.
"The wooing kestrel," I said, "mutes his mating-note
To please the harmony of this sweet silence."
And when at the day's end
We laid tired bodies 'gainst
The loose warm sands,
And the air fleeced its particles for a coverlet;
When star after star came out
To guard their lovers in oblivion—
My soul so leapt that my evening prayer
Stole my morning song!

—*Anne Spencer*

For Unity

God the Father,
source of Divinity,
good beyond all that is good,
fair beyond all that is fair,
in you is calmness, peace, and unity.
Repair the things that divide us from each other
and restore our unity of love
like your divine love.
And as you are above all things,
unite us in goodness and love
that we may be spiritually one,
with you and with each other,
through your peace which makes all things peaceful
and through the grace, mercy, and tenderness
of your only Son, Jesus Christ.
Amen.

—*Dionysius of the Syrian Jacobite Church, ninth century*

May Day

A delicate fabric of bird song
Floats in the air,
The smell of wet wild earth
Is everywhere.

Red small leaves of the maple
Are clenched like a hand,
Like girls at their first communion
The pear trees stand.

Oh I must pass nothing by
Without loving it much,
The raindrop try with my lips,
The grass with my touch;

For how can I be sure
I shall see again
The world on the first of May
Shining after the rain?

—*Sara Teasdale*

Kind Hearts

Kind hearts are the gardens,
Kind thoughts are the roots,
Kind words are the blossoms,
Kind deeds are the fruits;
Love is the sweet sunshine
That warms into life,
For only in darkness
Grow hatred and strife.

—*Anonymous*

Beauty

Even as on some black background full of night
And hollow storm in cloudy disarray,
The forceful brush of some great master may
More brilliantly evoke a higher light;
So beautiful, so delicately white,
So like a very metaphor of May,
Your loveliness on my life's sombre grey
In its perfection stands out doubly bright.

—*Blind*

How Would It Be?

How would it be
if just for today
we thought less about contests and rivalries,
profits and politics,
winners and sinners,
and more about
helping and giving,
mending and blending,
reaching out
and pitching in?
How would it be?

—Anonymous

The Way You See People

The way you see people is the way you treat them
and the way you treat them is what they become.

—Johann W. von Goethe

May All Creatures Be of a Blissful Heart

In safety and in Bliss
May all creatures be of a blissful heart
Whatever breathing beings there may be
Frail or firm…long or big…short or small
Seen or unseen, dwelling far or near

Existing or yet seeking to exist
May all creatures be of a blissful heart.

—*The Sutta Nipata*

Love Thy Neighbor

Lord Jesus, bind us to you and to our neighbor with love.
May our hearts not be turned away from you.
May our souls not be deceived nor our talents nor minds
enticed by allurements of error,
so that we may never distance ourselves from your love.
Thus may we love our neighbor as ourselves with strength,
wisdom, and gentleness. With your help, you who are blessed
throughout all ages.

—*Saint Anthony of Padua*

Do All the Good You Can

Do all the good you can,
By all the means you can,
In all the ways you can,
In all the places you can,
To all the people you can,
As long as ever you can.

—*John Wesley*

June

Rays of Sunshine

"We rise by lifting others."

—ROBERT INGERSOLL

"Nobody can be uncheered with a balloon."

—WINNIE THE POOH

"No act of kindness, no matter how small, is ever wasted."

—AESOP

"Service to others is the rent you pay
for your room here on earth."

—MUHAMMAD ALI

"Keep your face always toward the sunshine,
and the shadows will fall behind you."

—ADAGE FROM A WEST VIRGINIA PERIODICAL, 1862

"What sunshine is to flowers, smiles are to humanity."

—JOSEPH ADDISON

What Is Your Gift to the World?

May the gift I give
change me and our world.

—*Reverend Alan Claassen, 2011*

Prayer for the Illumination and Light

O Thou Who art generous and merciful!
We are the servants of Thy threshold and are gathered
beneath the sheltering shadow of Thy divine unity.
The sun of Thy mercy is shining upon all,
and the clouds of Thy bounty shower upon all.
Thy gifts encompass all,
Thy loving providence sustains all,
Thy protection overshadows all, and the glances of
Thy favor are cast upon all.
O Lord! Grant Thine infinite bestowals,
and let the light of Thy guidance shine.
Illumine the eyes, gladden the hearts with abiding joy.
Confer a new spirit upon all people and bestow
upon them eternal life.
Unlock the gates of true understanding
and let the light of faith shine resplendent.
Gather all people beneath the shadow of Thy bounty
and cause them to unite in harmony,
so that they may become as the rays of one sun,
as the waves of one ocean, and as the fruit of one tree.
May they be refreshed by the same breeze.

May they receive illumination from the same source of light.
Thou art the Giver, the Merciful, the Omnipotent.

—Byzantine Coptic Christian Prayer

Beloved Jesus, Shine Through Me Today

Dear Jesus, help us to spread your fragrance everywhere we go.
Flood our souls with your spirit and life.
Penetrate and possess our whole being so utterly
that our lives may only be a radiance of yours.
Shine through us, and be so in us
that every person we should come in contact with
may feel your presence in our soul.
Let them look up and see no longer us, but only Jesus.
Stay with us, and then we shall begin to shine as you shine;
so to shine as to be a light to others;
the light, Jesus, will be all from you.
None of it will be ours.
It will be you shining on others through us.
Let us thus praise you in the way you love best,
by shining on those around us.
Let us preach you without preaching:
not by words, but by our example,
by the catching force,
the sympathetic influence of what we do,
the evident fullness of the love our hearts bear for you.
Amen…

—Dr. Jane Goodall's favorite prayer, by Mother Teresa

You Never Walk Alone

Wherever I go, only Thou!
Wherever I stand, only Thou!
Just Thou, again Thou!
Always Thou!
Thou, Thou, Thou!
When things are good, Thou!
When things are bad, Thou!
Thou, Thou, Thou!

—Hasidic Ode

Lifting Up the Lowly

My soul proclaims the greatness of the Lord;
My spirit rejoices in God my savior.

For he has looked upon his handmaid's lowliness;
behold, from now on will all ages call me blessed.

The Mighty One has done great things for me,
and holy is his name.

His mercy is from age to age to those who fear him.

He has shown might with his arm,
dispersed the arrogant of mind and heart.

He has thrown down the rulers from their thrones
but lifted up the lowly.

The hungry he has filled with good things;
the rich he has sent away empty.

He has helped Israel his servant, remembering his mercy,
according to his promise to our fathers,
to Abraham and to his descendants forever.

—*Luke 1:46–55, CSB*

Coming Together—Growing Together

We light the light of a new idea.
It is the light of our coming together.
It is the light of our growing;
to know new things,
to see new beauty,
to feel new love.

—*Unitarian Chalice Lighting Invocation*

Making Life Worth While

Every soul that touches yours—
Be it the slightest contact—
Get there from some good;
Some little grace; one kindly thought;
One aspiration yet unfelt;
One bit of courage
For the darkening sky;
One gleam of faith
To brave the thickening ills of life;
One glimpse of brighter skies—
To make this life worthwhile
And heaven a surer heritage.

—*George Eliot (née Mary Ann Evans)*

Bring the Gift of Gladness to Others

Almighty God, thank Thee for the job of this day.
May we find gladness in all its toil and difficulty,
its pleasure and success,
and even in its failure and sorrow.
We would look always away from ourselves
and behold the glory and the need of the world
that we may have the will and the strength to bring
the gift of gladness to others;
that with them we stand to bear
the burden and heat of the day
and offer Thee the praise of work well done.
Amen.

—*Bishop Charles Lewis Slattery*

Shine Your Light and Share Your Light

Thousands of candles
can be lit from a single candle,
and the life of the candle
will not be shortened.
Happiness never decreases by being shared.

—*Buddha*

Enter into Soul-Light

Step into the Sunlight
Feel the pain wash away
Enter in the Soul-light
Just *be* in today.

Forget all emotion
Put your trust in the day
Let the past rush on by you
Put your Self in THE WAY.

—*Lynne Milum*

We Are All Under the Same Sun

The sun shines down,
and its image reflects a thousand
different pots filled with water.

The reflections are many,
but they are each reflecting the same sun.

Similarly, when we come to know who we truly are,
we will see ourselves in all people.

—*Amma*

The Sun Will Sometimes Melt a Field of Sorry

Sometimes things don't go, after all,
from bad to worse. Some years, muscadel
faces down frost; green thrives; the crops don't fail.
Sometimes a man aims high, and all goes well.

A people sometimes will step back from war,
elect an honest man, decide they care
enough, that they can't leave some stranger poor.
Some men become what they were born for.

Sometimes our best efforts do not go
amiss; sometimes we do as we meant to.
The sun will sometimes melt a field of sorrow
that seemed hard frozen; may it happen for you.

—*Sheenagh Pugh*

Keep on the Sunny Side of Life

There's a dark and a troubled side of life;
There's a bright and a sunny side, too;
Tho' we meet with the darkness and strife,
The sunny side we also may view.

Keep on the sunny side, always on the sunny side,
Keep on the sunny side of life;
It will help us every day, it will brighten all the way,
If we keep on the sunny side of life.

Tho' the storm in its fury break today,
Crushing hopes that we cherished so dear,
Storm and cloud will in time pass away,
The sun again will shine bright and clear.

Keep on the sunny side, always on the sunny side,
Keep on the sunny side of life;
It will help us every day, it will brighten all the way,
If we keep on the sunny side of life.

Let us greet with a song of hope each day,
Tho' the moments be cloudy or fair;
Let us trust in our Savior always,
Who keepeth everyone in His care.

Keep on the sunny side, always on the sunny side,
Keep on the sunny side of life;
It will help us every day, it will brighten all the way,
If we keep on the sunny side of life.

—Ada Blenkhorn, 1899

Lakota Prayer

Wakan Tanka, Great Mystery,
teach me how to trust
my heart,
my mind,
my intuition,
my inner knowing,
the senses of my body,
the blessings of my spirit.
Teach me to trust these things
so that I may enter my Sacred Space
and love beyond my fear,
and thus Walk in Balance
with the passing of each glorious Sun.

—Lakota Sioux Prayer

A Day of Sunshine

O gift of God! O perfect day:
Whereon shall no man work, but play;
Whereon it is enough for me,
Not to be doing, but to be!

Through every fibre of my brain,
Through every nerve, through every vein,
I feel the electric thrill, the touch
Of life, that seems almost too much.

I hear the wind among the trees
Playing celestial symphonies;
I see the branches downward bent,
Like keys of some great instrument.

And over me unrolls on high
The splendid scenery of the sky,
Where though a sapphire sea the sun
Sails like a golden galleon,

Toward yonder cloud-land in the West,
Toward yonder Islands of the Blest,
Whose steep sierra far uplifts
Its craggy summits white with drifts.

Blow, winds! and waft through all the rooms
The snow-flakes of the cherry-blooms!
Blow, winds! and bend within my reach
The fiery blossoms of the peach!

O Life and Love! O happy throng
Of thoughts, whose only speech is song!
O heart of man! canst thou not be
Blithe as the air is, and as free?

—*Henry Wadsworth Longfellow*

A Good Man

A good man never dies—
In worthy deed and prayer
And helpful hands, and honest eyes,
If smiles or tears be there:
Who lives for you and me—
Lives for the world he tries
To help—he lives eternally.
A good man never dies.

Who lives to bravely take
His share of toil and stress,
And, for his weaker fellows' sake,
Makes every burden less—
He may, at last, seem worn—
Lie fallen—hands and eyes
Folded—yet, though we mourn and mourn,
A good man never dies.

—*James Whitcomb Riley*

Psalm of the Day

A something in a summer's day,
As slow her flambeaux burn away,
Which solemnizes me.

A something in a summer's noon—
An azure depth, a wordless tune,
Transcending ecstasy.

And still within a summer's night
A something so transporting bright,
I clap my hands to see;

Then veil my too inspecting face,
Lest such a subtle, shimmering grace
Flutter too far for me.

The wizard-fingers never rest,
The purple brook within the breast
Still chafes its narrow bed;

Still rears the East her amber flag,
Guides still the sun along the crag
His caravan of red,

Like flowers that heard the tale of dews,
But never deemed the dripping prize
Awaited their low brows;

Or bees, that thought the summer's name
Some rumor of delirium
No summer could for them;

Or Arctic creature, dimly stirred
By tropic hint—some traveled bird
Imported to the wood;

Or wind's bright signal to the ear,
Making that homely and severe,
Contented, known, before

The heaven unexpected came,
To lives that thought their worshipping
A too presumptuous psalm.

—*Emily Dickinson*

The Gyatri Mantra

May my intellect be steady without agitation.
May it be clear without anger or passion.
May the brilliant light of the sun beam though my intellect so
that perception of the world may be clear, my discrimination
subtle, my judgment correct and quick, and my
comprehension of persons and situations precise and wise.

—*Hindu Mantra*

My Soul Is Awakened

My soul is awakened, my spirit is soaring,
And carried aloft on the wings of the breeze;
For above, and around me, the wild wind is roaring
Arousing to rapture the earth and the seas.

The long-withered grass in the sunshine is glancing,
The bare trees are tossing their branches on high;
The dead leaves beneath them are merrily dancing,
The white clouds are scudding across the blue sky.

I wish I could see how the ocean is lashing
The foam of its billows to whirlwinds of spray,
I wish I could see how its proud waves are dashing
And hear the wild roar of their thunder today!

—*Anne Brontë*

Renewal

As each day comes to us refreshed and anew, so
my gratitude renews itself daily. The breaking of the
sun over the horizon is my grateful heart dawning
upon a blessed world.

—*Terri Guillemets*

The Angels Dance

The angels dance in your wake
The sun rises for your glory
Stars illume in your light
Magnificent and eternal
My Lord Jesus
My timeless love

—*Justina M. Pernetter*

Arise, Shine!

Arise, Shine!
Arise, shine, for your light has come,
Arise, shine, for your light has come.
The glory of the Lord has risen
The glory of the Lord has come
The glory of the Lord has risen upon you.

—*Isaiah 60:1*

Have You Really Lived?

Love you not the tall trees spreading wide their branches,
Cooling with their green shade the sunny days of June?
Love you not the little bird lost among the leaflets,
Dreamily repeating a quaint, brief tune?

Is there not a joy in the waste windy places;
Is there not a song by the long dusty way?
Is there not a glory in the sudden hour of struggle?
Is there not a peace in the long quiet day?

Love you not the meadows with the deep lush grasses;
Love you not the cloud-flocks noiseless in their flight?
Love you not the cool wind that stirs to meet the sunrise;
Love you not the stillness of the warm summer night?

Have you never wept with a grief that slowly passes;
Have you never laughed when a joy goes running by?
Know you not the peace of rest that follows labor?
You have not learnt to live then; how can you dare to die?

—*Tertius Van Dyke*

The Flower at My Window

O! my heart now feels so cheerful as I go with footsteps light
In the daily toil of my dear home;
And I'll tell to you the secret that now
makes my life so bright—
There's a flower at my window in full bloom.

It is radiant in the sunshine, and so cheerful after rain;
And it wafts upon the air its sweet perfume.
It is very, very lovely! May its beauties never wane—
This dear flower at my window in full bloom.

Nature has so clothed it in such glorious array,
And it does so cheer our home, and hearts illume;
Its dear mem'ry I will cherish though the flower fade away—
This dear flower at my window in full bloom.

Oft I gaze upon this flower with its blossoms pure and white.
And I think as I behold its gay costume,
While through life we all are passing may
our lives be always bright
Like this flower at my window in full bloom.

—*Lucian B. Watkins*

Lift Up the Light of Your Face on Us

Eternal God,
uncreated and original Light,
Maker of all created things,
Fountain of pity, Sea of Bounty,
fathomless deep of Loving-Kindness,
lift up the light of your face on us!
Lord, shine in our hearts,
true Sun of Righteousness,
and fill our souls with your beauty.
Teach us always to remember your judgments,
and to speak of them,
and own you continually as our Lord and Friend.
Govern the works of our hands by your will,
and lead us in the right way,
that we may do what is pleasing and acceptable to you,
that through us unworthy people your holy name may
be glorified.
To you alone be praise and honor and worship eternally.
Amen.

—*St. Basil of Caesarea, fourth century*

The Fields of Light

When each day is sacred,
when each hour is sacred,
when each instant is sacred,
earth and you
space and you
bearing the sacred
through time,
you'll reach the fields of light.

—*Eugène Guillevic*

The Gladness of Nature

Is this a time to be cloudy and sad,
When our mother Nature laughs around;
When even the deep blue heavens look glad,
And gladness breathes from the blossoming ground?

There are notes of joy from the hang-bird and wren,
And the gossip of swallows through all the sky;
The ground-squirrel gaily chirps by his den,
And the wilding bee hums merrily by.

The clouds are at play in the azure space
And their shadows at play on the bright-green vale,
And here they stretch to the frolic chase,
And there they roll on the easy gale.

There's a dance of leaves in that aspen bower,
There's a titter of winds in that beechen tree,
There's a smile on the fruit, and a smile on the flower,
And a laugh from the brook that runs to the sea.

And look at the broad-faced sun, how he smiles
On the dewy earth that smiles in his ray,
On the leaping waters and gay young isles;
Ay, look, and he'll smile thy gloom away.

—*William Cullen Bryant*

All Treasures

Spirit of truth,
you are the reward to the saints,
the comforter of souls,
light in the darkness,
riches to the poor,
treasure to lovers,
food for the hungry,
comfort to the wanderer;
to sum up,
you are the one in whom all treasures are contained.

—*Saint Mary Magdalen dei Pazzi*

Give Me Light

O God, give me, I pray Thee,
light on my right hand
and light on my left hand
and light above me
and light beneath me,
O Lord, increase light within me
and give me light
and illuminate me.

—*Muhammad (circa AD 570–632)*

Like a Wildflower

May your life be like a wildflower
growing freely in the beauty and joy of each day.

—*Native American Proverb*

July

Breaking New Ground

"No matter how hard the past is, you can always begin again."

—BUDDHA

"Doubt kills more dreams than failure ever will."

—SUZY KASSEM

"The best way to predict the future is to invent it."

**—NIGEL CALDER IN *NEW SCIENTIST*, 1963,
AFTER DENNIS GABOR'S WORK
INVENTING THE FUTURE (1963)**

"It's what you learn after you know it all that counts."

—HARRY S. TRUMAN

"Many of life's failures are people who did not realize how close they were to success when they gave up."

—THOMAS EDISON

"It's fun to do the impossible."

—WALT DISNEY

The Optimist's Creed

To be so strong that nothing
can disturb your peace of mind.

To talk health, happiness, and prosperity
to every person you meet.

To make all your friends feel
that there is something in them.

To look at the sunny side of everything
and make your optimism come true.

To think only the best, to work only for the best,
and to expect only the best.

To be just as enthusiastic about the success of others
as you are about your own.

To forget the mistakes of the past
and press on to the greater achievements of the future.

To wear a cheerful countenance at all times
and give every living creature you meet a smile.

To give so much time to the improvement of yourself
that you have no time to criticize others.

To be too large for worry, too noble for anger,
too strong for fear,
and too happy to permit the presence of trouble.

To think well of yourself and to proclaim this fact to the world,
not in loud words but with great deeds.

To live in faith that the whole world is on your side
so long as you are true to the best that is in you.

—*Christian D. Larson, 1912*

It Is

It's the little bit of sunshine
Lighting up the dullest day,
That brings a glow of pleasure
As we journey on Life's way.
It's the simple things that please us
Like a willing kindness done,
That son blow away each storm-cloud
'Till once more we see the sun.

—*John McLeod*

You Are Guided, Guarded, and Protected

The light of God surrounds me;
The love of God enfolds me;
The power of God protects me;
The presence of God watches over me.
Wherever I am, God is.

—*James Dillet Freeman, 1941*

Light the Light of a New Idea

We light the light of a new idea.
It is the light of our coming together.
It is the light of our growing;
to know new things,
to see new beauty,
to feel new love.

—*Invocation*

Hope

Hope is the thing with feathers
That perches in the soul
And sings the tune without the words
And never stops at all
And sweetest in the Gale is heard
And sore must be the storm
That could abash the little bird
That kept so many warm
I've heard it in the chillest land
And on the strangest sea
Yet, never, in extremity,
It asked a crumb of me.

—*Emily Dickinson*

Hope

Our lives, discoloured with our present woes,
May still grow white and shine with happier hours.
So the pure limpid stream, when foul with stains
Of rushing torrents and descending rains,
Works itself clear, and as it runs refines,
till by degrees the floating mirror shines;
Reflects each flower that on the border grows,
And a new heaven in its fair bosom shows.

—*Joseph Addison*

Unity

I dreamed that life and time and space were one,
And the pure trance of dawn;
The increase drawn
From all the journeys of the traveling sun,
And the long mysteries of sound and sight,
The whispering rains,
And far, calm waters set in lonely plains,
And cry of birds at night.

I dreamed that these and love and death were one,
And all eternity,
The life to be
Therewith entwined, throughout the ages spun;
And so with Grief, my playmate; him I knew
One with the rest—
One with the mounting day, the east and west—

Lord, is it true?
Lord, do I dream? Methinks a key unlocks
Some dungeon door, in thrall of blackened towers,
On ecstasies, half hid, like chill white flowers
Blown in the secret places of the rocks.

—Violet Jacob

Find Something Better in Your Future

A very wise man once told me
that you can't look back—
you just have to put the past behind you
and find something better in your future.

—Jodi Picoult

The Rainbow

Soft falls the shower, the thunders cease!
And see the messenger of peace
Illumes the eastern skies;
Blest sign of firm unchanging love!
While others seek the cause to prove,
That bids thy beauties rise.

My soul, content with humbler views,
Well pleased admires thy varied hues,
And can with joy behold
Thy beauteous form, and wondering gaze
Enraptured on thy mingled rays
Of purple, green, and gold.

Enough for me to deem divine
The hand that paints each glowing line;
To think that thou art given
A transient gleam of that bright place
Where Beauty owns celestial grace,
A faint display of Heaven!

—*Charlotte Richardson*

Help My Eyes to See

Jesus, help my eyes to see
All the good Thou sendest me.
Jesus, help my ears to hear
Calls for help from far and near.
Jesus, help my feet to go
In the way that Thou wilt show.
Jesus, help my hands to do
All things loving, kind, and true.
Jesus, may I helpful be,
Growing every day like Thee.
Amen.

—*Anonymous*

Becoming the Ocean

It is said that before entering the sea
a river trembles with fear.
She looks back at the path she has traveled,
from the peaks of the mountains,
the long winding road crossing forests and villages.
And in front of her,
she sees an ocean so vast,
that to enter
there seems nothing more than to disappear forever.
But there is no other way.
The river cannot go back.
Nobody can go back.
To go back is impossible in existence.
The river needs to take the risk
of entering the ocean
because only then will fear disappear,
because that's where the river will know
it's not about disappearing into the ocean,
but of becoming the ocean.

—*Khalil Gibran*

Guide Us When the Way Is Uncertain

Good Shepherd, guide us
when the way is uncertain
and the path overgrown,
back onto higher ground
from where we might see,
behind us, the place from which
you have patiently brought us,
and ahead of us once more
glimpse your footsteps
leading forward, into which
we will try and place our own.

—*Celtic Prayer of Approach*

Show Me Your Ways

Show me your ways, Lord,
teach me your paths.
Guide me in your truth and teach me.

—*Psalm 25:4–5 NIV*

Envy

This rose-tree is not made to bear
The violet blue, nor lily fair,
Nor the sweet mignionette:
And if this tree were discontent,
Or wished to change its natural bent,
It all in vain would fret.
And should it fret, you would suppose

It ne'er had seen its own red rose,
Nor after gentle shower
Had ever smelled its rose's scent,
Or it could ne'er be discontent
With its own pretty flower.

Like such a blind and senseless tree
As I've imagined this to be,
All envious persons are:
With care and culture all may find
Some pretty flower in their own mind,
Some talent that is rare.

—*Mary Lamb*

My Life's Delight

Come, O come, my life's delight,
Let me not in languor pine!
Love loves no delay; thy sight,
The more enjoyed, the more divine:
O come, and take from me
The pain of being deprived of thee!

Thou all sweetness dost enclose,
Like a little world of bliss.
Beauty guards thy looks: the rose
In them pure and eternal is.
Come, then, and make thy flight
As swift to me as heavenly light.

—*Thomas Campion*

May Your Will Be Done

Lord, grant that I may always allow myself
to be guided by you,
always follow your plans, and perfectly
accomplish your holy will.
Grant that in all things, great and small, today
and all the days of my life,
I may do whatever you require of me.
Help me to respond to the slightest prompting of your grace,
so that I may be your trustworthy instrument for your honor.
May your will be done in time and eternity by me, in me, and
through me.
Amen.

—*Saint Teresa of Avila*

Let Me Not Lose My Dream

Let me not lose my dream, e'en though I scan the veil
with eyes unseeing through their glaze of tears,
Let me not falter, though the rungs of fortune perish
as I fare above the tumult, praying purer air,
Let me not lose the vision, gird me. Powers that toss
the worlds, I pray!
Hold me, and guard, lest anguish tear my dreams away!

—*Georgia Douglas Johnson*

A Far Country

Beyond the cities I have seen,
Beyond the wrack and din,
There is a wide and fair demesne
Where I have never been.

Away from desert wastes of greed,
Over the peaks of pride,
Across the seas of mortal need
Its citizens abide.

And through the distance though I see
How stern must be the fare,
My feet are ever fain to be
Upon the journey there.

In that far land the only school
The dwellers all attend
Is built upon the Golden Rule,
And man to man is friend.

No war is there nor war's distress,
But truth and love increase—
It is a realm of pleasantness,
And all her paths are peace.

—*Leslie Pinckney Hill*

Walk with Us

Jesus our Master,
walk with us on the road
as we yearn to reach the heavenly country,
so that following your light,
we may stay on the way of righteousness,
and never wander
into the horrible darkness of this world's night,
while you, the way, the truth, and the life,
are shining within us.

—*Mozarabic Rite*

Enlighten Our Meditations

O our Lord and God,
enlighten our meditations
that we may hear and understand
your life-giving and divine commands.
Through your grace and mercy
assure us of your love, hope,
and salvation of soul and body,
and we shall sing to you
everlasting glory forever,
O Lord of all.
Amen.

—*Liturgy of the Blessed Apostles, fifth century*

The Days to Come

Now shall I store my soul with silent beauty,
Beauty of drifting clouds and mountain heights,
Beauty of sun-splashed hills and shadowed forests,
Beauty of dawn and dusk and star-swept nights.

Now shall I fill my heart with quiet music,
Song of the wind across the pine-clad hill,
Song of the rain and, fairer than all music,
Call of the thrush when twilight woods are still.

So shall the days to come be filled with beauty,
Bright with the promise caught from eastern skies;
So shall I see the stars when night is darkest,
Still hear the thrush's song when music dies.

—*Medora C. Addison*

Guide Our Souls

O God, be present with us always,
dwell within our hearts.
With your light and your Spirit
guide our souls, our thoughts, and all our actions,
that we may teach your Word,
that your healing power may be in us
and in your church universal.
Amen.

—*Philip Melanchthon*

Help Yourself to Happiness

Everybody, everywhere seeks happiness, it's true,
But finding it and keeping it seem difficult to do.
Difficult because we think that happiness is found
Only in the places where wealth and fame abound—
And so we go on searching in palaces of pleasure
Seeking recognition and monetary treasure,
Unaware that happiness is just a state of mind
Within the reach of everyone who takes time to be kind.
For in making others happy, we will be happy, too.
For the happiness you give away returns to shine on you.

—Helen Steiner Rice

Eternity in an Hour

To see a World in a Grain of Sand
And a Heaven in a Wild Flower
Hold Infinity in the palm of your hand
And Eternity in an hour

—William Blake

Avoiding Anxiety

No amount of anxiety makes any difference to
anything that is going to happen.

—*Alan Watts*

The Smaller Things

If I cannot do great things, I can do small things in a great way.

—*Dr. Martin Luther King Jr.*

Make Us Fearless

From that which we fear, make us fearless.
O bounteous One, assist us with your aid.
May the atmosphere we breathe
breathe fearlessness into us;
fearlessness on earth
and fearlessness in heaven!
May fearlessness surround us
above and below!
May we be without fear
by night and by day!
Let all the night be my friend!

—*Atharva Veda XIX*

Within Our Reach

There is nothing I can give you
which you do have not;
But there is much, very much, that
while I cannot give it, you can take.
No heaven can come to us unless our hearts
find rest in today. Take heaven!
No peace lies in the future which is not hidden
in this present instant. Take peace!
The gloom of the world is but a shadow.
Behind it, yet within reach, is joy.
There is a radiance and glory in the darkness, could
we but see,
and to see, we have only to look. I beseech you
to look.

—*Fra Giovanni*

Life Renewing

Earth, ourselves,
breathe and awaken,
leaves are stirring,
all things moving,
new day coming,
life renewing.

—*Pawnee Prayer*

The Plans I Have for You

For I know the plans I have for you,
declares the Lord,
plans to prosper you and not to harm you,
plans to give you hope and a future.

—*Jeremiah 29:11 (NIV)*

Commit to the Lord

Commit to the Lord whatever you do,
and your plans will succeed.

—*Proverbs 16:3 (GNV)*

August

The Sky's the Limit

"The creation of a thousand forests is in one acorn."
—RALPH WALDO EMERSON

"Everyone wants to live on top of the mountain, but all the happiness and growth occurs while you're climbing it."
—ANDY ROONEY

"The miraculous is the least one must aim at."
—MARY BURCHELL

"Any crusade requires optimism and the ambition to aim high."
—PAUL ALLEN

"There is nothing impossible to him who will try."
—ALEXANDER THE GREAT

"You are never too old to set another goal or to dream a new dream."
—C.S. LEWIS

What Doesn't Kill You Makes You Stronger

God does not send us despair in order to kill us; he
sends it in order to awaken us to new life.

—*Hermann Hesse in Reflections*

Believe More Deeply

Believe more deeply.
Hold your face up to the light,
even though for the moment you do not see.

—*Bill Wilson, Cofounder of Alcoholics Anonymous*

Seek and Ye Shall Find

Ask, and it shall be given you;
Seek, and you shall find;
Knock, and it shall be opened to you.
For whoever asks, receives;
And he who seeks, finds;
And to him who knocks, the door is opened.

—*Matthew 7:7, The Words of Christ, NIV*

Never Give Up

I will not die an unlived life.
I will not live in fear
of falling or catching fire.
I choose to inhabit my days,
to allow my living to open me,
to make me less afraid,
more accessible,
to loosen my heart
until it becomes a wing.

—*Dawna Markova*

Persist

When things go wrong, as they sometimes will,
When the road you're trudging seems all uphill,
When the funds are low and the debts are high,
And you want to smile, but you have to sigh,
When care is pressing you down a bit,
Rest, if you must—but don't you quit.
Life is queer with its twists and turns,
As every one of us sometimes learns,
And many a failure turns about,
When he might have won had he stuck it out,
Don't give up, though the pace seems slow…
You might succeed with another blow.
Often the goal is nearer than
It seems to a faint and faltering man.
Often the struggler has given up,
When he might have captured the victor's cup,
And he learned too late, when the night slipped down,

How close he was to the golden crown.
Success is failure turned inside out,
The silver tint to the clouds of doubt—
And you can never tell how close you are,
It may appear when it seems afar;
So stick to the fight when you're hardest hit—
It's when things seem worst that you mustn't quit!

—Anonymous

❧

Keep Looking for Those Silver Linings

If you want the rainbow, you have to put up with the rain.

—Dolly Parton

❧

Rid Your Brain of Negativity

Life's too short to simply waste,
Slow it down, don't move with haste.
Time is once, you get to spend,
Carefully choose every friend.

Life's too short to change careers,
Choice is yours, they're your years.
Maybe once, or maybe twice,
Look inside to find advice.

Life's too short, to just complain,
Rid negativity from your brain.
Life's too short, time won't freeze,
Enjoy it all, won't you please.

—Anonymous

How Can We Be Our Best Selves

Great God, who has told us
"Vengeance is mine,"
save us from ourselves,
save us from the vengeance in our hearts
and the acid in our souls.

Save us from our desire to hurt as we have been hurt,
to punish as we have been punished,
to terrorize as we have been terrorized.

Give us the strength it takes
to listen rather than to judge,
to trust rather than to fear,
to try again and again
to make peace even when peace eludes us.

We ask, O God, for the grace
to be our best selves.
We ask for the vision
to be builders of the human community
rather than its destroyers.
We ask for the humility as a people
to understand the fears and hopes of other peoples.

We ask for the love it takes
to bequeath to the children of the world to come
more than the failures of our own making.
We ask for the heart it takes.

—*Sister Joan Chittister*

Becoming Your Best You

Close your eyes
and imagine the best
version of you possible.
That's who you really are.
Let go of any part of you
that doesn't believe it.

—C. Assaid

Never Give In!

When things go wrong, as they sometimes will,
when the road you're trudging seems all uphill,
when the funds are low and the debts are high,
and you want to smile, but you have to sigh,
when care is pressing you down a bit,
rest, if you must—but don't you quit.

Life is queer with its twists and turns,
as every one of us sometimes learns,
and many a fellow turns about,
when he might have won had he stuck it out.
Don't give up, though the pace seems slow…
You might succeed with another blow.

Often the goal is nearer than it seems
to a faint and faltering man.
Often the struggler has given up,
when he might have captured the victor's cup,
and learned too late when the night slipped down,
How close he was to the golden crown.

Success is failure turned inside out,
the silver tint to the clouds of doubt—
And you can never tell how close you are.
It may appear when it seems afar;
So stick to the fight when you're hardest hit—
It's when things seem worst that you mustn't quit!

—*Anonymous*

What Is Stopping You?

The brick walls are there for a reason.
The brick walls are not there to keep us out.
The brick walls are there to give us a chance
to show how badly we want something.
Because the brick walls are there
to stop the people who don't want it badly enough.
They're there to stop the other people.

—*Randy Pausch*

You Must Do the Thing You Think You Cannot Do

You gain strength, courage, and confidence
by every experience in which you really
stop to look fear in the face.

You are able to say to yourself, "I have
lived through this horror.
I can take the next thing that comes along."
You must do the thing you think you cannot do.

—*Eleanor Roosevelt*

Flight of the Eagle

Through the storm the eagle flies,
He knows today, he lives and dies.
For his steel, the bright and true,
hammering blows to forge the new,
Red the sky, at dawn tomorrow,
Strong! his cry, no tears of sorrow.

—*Ancient Norse Poem*

A Summer Afternoon

A languid atmosphere, a lazy breeze,
With labored respiration, moves the wheat
From distant reaches, till the golden seas
Break in crisp whispers at my feet.

My book, neglected of an idle mind,
Hides for a moment from the eyes of men;
Or lightly opened by a critic wind,
Affrightedly reviews itself again.

Off through the haze that dances in the shine
The warm sun showers in the open glade,
The forest lies, a silhouette design
Dimmed through and through with shade.

A dreamy day; and tranquilly I lie
At anchor from all storms of mental strain;
With absent vision, gazing at the sky,
Like one that hears it rain.

The Katydid, so boisterous last night,
　Clinging, inverted, in uneasy poise,
Beneath a wheat-blade, has forgotten quite
　If "Katy *did* or *didn't*" make a noise.

The twitter, sometimes, of a wayward bird
　That checks the song abruptly at the sound,
And mildly, chiding echoes that have stirred,
　Sink into silence, all the more profound.

And drowsily I hear the plaintive strain
　Of some poor dove… Why, I can scarcely keep
My heavy eyelids—there it is again—
"Coo-coo!"—I mustn't—"Coo-coo!"—fall asleep!

—*James Whitcomb Riley*

Victory

Do not seek too much fame,
　but do not seek obscurity.
Be proud.
But do not remind the world of your deeds.
Excel when you must,
　but do not excel the world.
Many heroes are not yet born,
　many have already died.
To be alive to hear this song is a victory.

—*West African Song*

By the Strength of My Motivation

By the strength of my pure motivation,
Coupled with the power of the Realized Ones,
And the mystic force of the Dharmadhatu,
May all the aims that we have in mind,
That accord with the laws of Truth
Occur without obstruction.

—*Nagarjuna*

Cloud Thoughts

Above the clouds I sail, above the clouds,
And wish my mind
Above its clouds could climb as well,
And leave behind
The world and all its crowds,
And ever dwell
In such a calm and limpid solitude
With ne'er a breath unkind or harsh or rude
To break the spell—
With ne'er a thought to drive away
The golden splendour of the day.
Alone and lost beneath the tranquil blue,
My God! With you!

—*Paul Bewsher*

Patience of Hope

The flowers that bloom in sun and shade
And glitter in the dew,
The flowers must fade.
The birds that build their nest and sing
When lovely spring is new,
Must soon take wing.

The sun that rises in his strength
To wake and warm the world,
Must set at length.
The sea that overflows the shore
With billows frothed and curled,
Must ebb once more.

All come and go, all wax and wane,
O Lord, save only Thou
Who dost remain
The same to all eternity.
All things which fail us now
We trust to Thee.

—*Christina Georgina Rossetti*

Twenty Years

Twenty years from now you will be more disappointed
by the things that you didn't do
than by the ones you did do.
So throw off the bowlines.
Sail away from the safe harbor.
Catch the trade winds in your sails.
Explore, dream, discover.

—*Sarah Frances Brown*

See It Through

When you're up against a trouble,
Meet it squarely, face to face;
Lift your chin and set your shoulders,
Plant your feet and take a brace.
When it's vain to try to dodge it,
Do the best that you can do;
You may fail, but you may conquer,
See it through!

Black may be the clouds about you
And your future may seem grim,
But don't let your nerve desert you;
Keep yourself in fighting trim.
If the worst is bound to happen,
Spite of all that you can do,
Running from it will not save you,
See it through!

Even hope may seem but futile,
When with troubles you're beset,
But remember you are facing
Just what other men have met.
You may fail, but fall still fighting;
Don't give up, whate'er you do;
Eyes front, head high to the finish.
See it through!

—Edgar Guest

Benediction

Go forth, my son,
Winged by my heart's desire!
Great reaches, yet unknown,
Await
For your possession.
I may not, if I would,
Retrace the way with you,
My pilgrimage is through,
But life is calling you!
Fare high and far, my son,
A new day has begun,
Thy star-ways must be won!

—Georgia Douglas Johnson

Do Not Quit

It does not matter how slowly you go
as long as you do not stop.

—Confucius

The Value of Inspiration

When you are inspired by some great purpose,
some extraordinary project,
all your thoughts break their bonds.

—Patanjali

The Joy of Achievement

Happiness lies in the joy of achievement
and the thrill of creative effort.

—Franklin D. Roosevelt

God the Artist

God, when you chiseled a raindrop,
How did you think of a stem,
Bearing a lovely satin leaf
To hold the tiny gem?

—Angela Morgan

Be the Best of Whatever You Are

If you can't be a pine on the top of the hill,
Be a scrub in the valley—but be
The best little scrub by the side of the rill;
Be a bush if you can't be a tree.

If you can't be a bush be a bit of the grass,
And some highway happier make;
If you can't be a muskie then just be a bass—
But the liveliest bass in the lake!

We can't all be captains, we've got to be crew,
There's something for all of us here,
There's big work to do, and there's lesser to do,
And the task you must do is the near.

If you can't be a highway then just be a trail,
If you can't be the sun be a star;
It isn't by size that you win or you fail—
Be the best of whatever you are!

—*Douglas Malloch*

To Be Nobody but Yourself

To be nobody-but-yourself
in a world which is doing its best day and night
to make you like everybody else
means to fight the hardest battle
which any human being can fight,
and never stop fighting.

—*e.e. cummings*

Success in Failure

Success is walking from failure to failure with no loss
of enthusiasm.

—*Winston Churchill*

Experiencing Life

Life is not a problem to be solved but a reality to
be experienced.

—*Søren Kierkegaard*

Simplicity Is Key

It's strange how simple things become, once you see
them clearly.

—*Ayn Rand*

Seeing Through the Hourglass of Life

The more sand had escaped from the hourglass of our life, the
clearer we should see through it.

—*Niccolo Machiavelli*

September

The Road That Leads Ahead

"Keep walking through the storm. Your
rainbow is waiting on the other side."

—HEATHER STILLUFSEN

"Look with favour upon a bold beginning."

—VIRGIL

"Let yourself be silently drawn by the strange pull of
what you really love. It will not lead you astray."

—JALAL AL-DIN RUMI

"Follow your bliss and the universe will open
doors where there were only walls."

—JOSEPH CAMPBELL

"Success is not final; failure is not fatal: it is
the courage to continue that counts."

—GEORGE F. TILTON IN *FORBES* MAGAZINE, 1948

"There are no traffic jams along the extra mile."

—ROGER STAUBACH

May We Always Be Ready for the Long Journey

O, our Father the Sky, hear us
and make us strong.
O, our Mother the Earth, hear us
and give us support.
O Spirit of the East,
send us your Wisdom.
O Spirit of the South,
may we tread your path.
O Spirit of the West,
may we always be ready for the long journey.
O Spirit of the North, purify us
with your cleansing winds.

—*Oglala Sioux Tribal Chant*

All Roads Lead to the Same Great Truth

I believe in the fundamental truth of all
great religions of the world.
I believe that they are all God-given
and I believe that they were necessary
for the people to whom these religions were revealed.
And I believe that if only we could all of us
read the scriptures of the different faiths from the standpoints
of the followers of these faiths,
we should find that they were at bottom
all one and were all helpful to one another.

—*Mahatma Gandhi*

The Soul's Passage

Exultation is the going
Of an inland soul to sea,
Past the houses—past the headlands—
Into deep Eternity—
Bred as we, among the mountains,
Can the sailor understand
The divine intoxication
Of the first league out from land?

—Emily Dickinson

Walking with the Lord

Lord, take me where You want me to go;
Let me meet who You want me to meet;
Tell me what You want me to say; and
Keep me out of your way.

—Father Mechal Judge, FDNY—Died 9/11/01

Happiness Is the Way

You should be happy right in the here and now.
There is no way to enlightenment.
Enlightenment should be right here and right now.
The moment when you come back to yourself,
mind and body together,
fully present, fully alive,
that is already enlightenment…
You are fully alive.
You are awake.
Enlightenment is there.
And if you continue each moment like that,
enlightenment becomes deeper.

—*Thich Nhat Hanh*

The Lamp of Life

Always we are following a light,
Always the light recedes; with groping hands
We stretch toward this glory, while the lands
We journey through are hidden from our sight
Dim and mysterious, folded deep in night,
We care not, all our utmost need demands
Is but the light, the light! So still it stands
Surely our own if we exert our might.
Fool! Never can'st thou grasp this fleeting gleam,
Its glowing flame would die if it were caught,

Its value is that it doth always seem
But just a little farther on. Distraught,
But lighted ever onward, we are brought
Upon our way unknowing, in a dream.

—Amy Lowell

Strength for the Journey

My True Father,
I set my hopes upon You alone,
And I only ask You, God,
For my Soul salvation.

Let Your Holy Will
Be my strengthening on this way,
For my life without You is a mere empty moment,
And only serving You leads to Eternal life.
Amen.

—St. Agapit of Pechersk, eleventh century

The Soul Walks All Paths

The hidden well-spring of your soul must needs
rise and run murmuring to the sea;
And the treasure of your infinite depths
would be revealed to your eyes.
But let there be no scales to weigh your unknown treasure;
And seek not the depths of your knowledge
with staff or sounding line.
For self is a sea boundless and measureless.
Say not, "I have found the truth,"
but rather, "I have found a truth."
Say not, "I have found the path of the soul."
Say rather, "I have met the soul walking upon my path."
For the soul walks upon all paths.
The soul walks not upon a line, neither does it grow like a reed.
The soul unfolds itself, like a lotus of countless petals.

—*Kahlil Gibran*

We Are on the Same Path

Religions are different roads
converging upon the same point.
What does it matter
that we take different roads
so long as we reach the same goal.

—*Mahatma Gandhi*

Facing the Future

Every journey begins
With but a small step.
And every day is a chance
For a new, small step
In the right direction.
Just follow your Heartsong.

—*Mattie J. Stepanek*

On This Long, Rough Road

Promise me,
promise me this day,
promise me now,
while the sun is overhead
exactly at the zenith,
promise me:

Even as they
strike you down
with a mountain of hatred and violence;
even as they step on you and crush you
like a worm,
even as they dismember and disembowel you,
remember, brother,
remember:
man is not our enemy.

The only thing worthy of you is compassion—
invincible, limitless, unconditional.
Hatred will never let you face
the beast in man.

One day, when you face this beast alone,
with your courage intact, your eyes kind,
untroubled
(even as no one sees them),
out of your smile
will bloom a flower.

And those who love you
will behold you
across ten thousand worlds of birth and dying.

Alone again,
I will go on with bent head,
knowing that love has become eternal.
On the long, rough road,
the sun and the moon
will continue to shine.

—*Thích Nhất Hạnh*

You Can Do Anything

Start by doing what's necessary;
then do what's possible;
and suddenly
you are doing the impossible.

—*attributed to Saint Francis of Assisi*

Peace in Every Step

God be between you and harm in
all the empty places you walk.

—Egyptian Blessing, 172

Surrounded by Beauty

Your feet I walk
I walk with your limbs
I carry forth your body
For me your mind thinks
Your voice speaks for me
Beauty is before me
And beauty is behind me
Above and below me hovers the beautiful
I am surrounded by it
I am immersed in it
In my youth I am aware of it
And in old age I shall walk quietly
The beautiful trail.

—Navajo Chant

Uphill

Does the road wind uphill all the way?
Yes, to the very end.
Will the day's journey take the whole long day?
From morn to night, my friend.
But is there for the night a resting-place?
A roof for when the slow dark hours begin.
May not the darkness hide it from my face?
You cannot miss that inn.
Shall I meet other wayfarers at night?
Those who have gone before.
Then must I knock, or call when just in sight?
They will not keep you standing at that door.
Shall I find comfort, travel-sore and weak?
Of labour you shall find the sum.
Will there be beds for me and all who seek?
Yea, beds for all who come.

—*Christina Rossetti 1830–1894*

The First Step

Take the first step in faith
You don't have to see the whole staircase,
Just take the first step.

—Dr. Martin Luther King, Jr.

Nothing Can Destroy Him

On life's journey, faith is nourishment,
virtuous deeds are a shelter,
wisdom is the light by day
and right mindfulness is the protection by night.
If a man lives a pure life,
nothing can destroy him.

—Buddha

Follow Diligently

Follow diligently the Way in your own heart,
but make no display of it to the world.
Keep behind, and you shall be put in front;
keep out, and you shall be kept in.
He that humbles himself shall be preserved entire.
He that bends shall be made straight.
He that is empty shall be filled.
He that is worn out shall be renewed.

—Lao-Tse

Take My Hand

Precious Lord, take my hand.
Lead me on. Let me stand.
I am tired. I am weak. I am worn.
Through the storm,
Through the night,
Lead me on to the light.
Take my hand, precious Lord,
and lead me home.

—*The United Methodist Hymnal, No. 474*

The Door Will Be Opened

The door will be opened to anyone who knocks.

—*Luke 11:10*

The Walk

A Queen rejoices in her peers,
And wary Nature knows her own
By court and city, dale and down,
And like a lover volunteers,
And to her son will treasures more
And more to purpose freely pour
In one wood walk, than learned men
Can find with glass in ten times ten.

—*Ralph Waldo Emerson*

A Great and Boundless Realm

Jesus said,

Come, that I may teach you about
secrets no person has ever seen.
For there exists a great and boundless realm,
whose extent no generation of angels has seen,
in which there is a great invisible Spirit,
which no eye of an angel has ever seen,
no thought of the heart has ever comprehended,
and it was never called by any name.

—The Gospel of Judas, second century

The Road Ahead

My Lord God,

I have no idea where I am going
I do not see the road ahead of me.
I cannot know for certain where it will end.

Nor do I really know myself,
And the fact that I think I am following
your will does not mean that I am
actually doing so.

But I believe that the desire to please
you does in fact please you.
And I hope that I have that desire in all
that I am doing.
And I know that if I do this, you
will lead me by the right road
though I may know nothing about it.

Therefore I will trust you always
though I may seem to be lost
and in the shadow of death, I will
not fear, for you are ever with me
and you will never leave me
to face my perils alone.

—*Thomas Merton*

Travel

The railroad track is miles away,
And the day is loud with voices speaking,
Yet there isn't a train goes by all day
But I hear its whistle shrieking.

All night there isn't a train goes by,
Though the night is still for sleep and dreaming
But I see its cinders red on the sky,
And hear its engine steaming.

My heart is warm with the friends I make,
And better friends I'll not be knowing,
Yet there isn't a train I wouldn't take,
No matter where it's going.

—*Edna St. Vincent Millay*

The Road Not Taken

Two roads diverged in a yellow wood,
And sorry I could not travel both
And be one traveler, long I stood
And looked down one as far as I could
To where it bent in the undergrowth;

Then took the other, as just as fair,
And having perhaps the better claim
Because it was grassy and wanted wear,
Though as for that the passing there
Had worn them really about the same,

And both that morning equally lay
In leaves no step had trodden black.
Oh, I marked the first for another day!
Yet knowing how way leads on to way
I doubted if I should ever come back.

I shall be telling this with a sigh
Somewhere ages and ages hence:
Two roads diverged in a wood, and I,
I took the one less traveled by,
And that has made all the difference.

—Robert Frost

Journey

Ah, could I lay me down in this long grass
And close my eyes, and let the quiet wind
Blow over me—I am so tired, so tired
Of passing pleasant places! All my life,
Following Care along the dusty road,
Have I looked back at loveliness and sighed;
Yet at my hand an unrelenting hand
Tugged ever, and I passed. All my life long
Over my shoulder have I looked at peace;
And now I fain would lie in this long grass
And close my eyes.
Yet onward!
Cat birds call
Through the long afternoon, and creeks at dusk
Are guttural. Whip-poor-wills wake and cry,
Drawing the twilight close about their throats.
Only my heart makes answer. Eager vines
Go up the rocks and wait; flushed apple-trees
Pause in their dance and break the ring for me;
Dim, shady wood-roads, redolent of fern
And bayberry, that through sweet bevies thread
Of round-faced roses, pink and petulant,
Look back and beckon ere they disappear.
Only my heart, only my heart responds.
Yet, ah, my path is sweet on either side
All through the dragging day—sharp underfoot
And hot, and like dead mist the dry dust hangs—

But far, oh, far as passionate eye can reach,
And long, ah, long as rapturous eye can cling,
The world is mine: blue hill, still silver lake,
Broad field, bright flower, and the long white road
A gateless garden, and an open path:
My feet to follow, and my heart to hold.

—Edna St. Vincent Millay

Direct Our Ways

O almighty and eternal God,
mercifully direct our ways
that we may walk in your law
and abound in good works;
through your beloved Son,
Jesus Christ our Lord,
who lives and reigns
with you and the Holy Spirit,
one true God, now and forever.
Amen.

—Veit Dietrich

Give Sight to All

God of the journey,
  give sight to all
who have not found
  the path to follow,
  strength to those
  who are walking
the path that you have trod,
  and hope to those
  growing weary
  of the traveling,
  that all might meet
  one glorious day
at this journey's end.

—*Author Unknown*

Dream Song

It is I who travel in the winds,
It is I who whisper in the breeze,
I shake the trees,
I shake the earth,
I trouble the waters on every land.

—*Ojibwa tradition*

Over the Hills and Far Away

Where forlorn sunsets flare and fade
On desolate sea and lonely sand,
Out of the silence and the shade
What is the voice of strange command
Calling you still, as friend calls friend
With love that cannot brook delay,
To rise and follow the ways that wend
Over the hills and far away?

Hark in the city, street on street
A roaring reach of death and life,
Of vortices that clash and fleet
And ruin in appointed strife,
Hark to it calling, calling clear,
Calling until you cannot stay
From dearer things than your own most dear
Over the hills and far away.

Out of the sound of the ebb-and-flow,
Out of the sight of lamp and star,
It calls you where the good winds blow,
And the unchanging meadows are;
From faded hopes and hopes agleam,
It calls you, calls you night and day
Beyond the dark into the dream
Over the hills and far away.

—*William Ernest Henley*

October

Turning Over a New Leaf

"What you feed your mind will lead your life."
—KEMI SOGUNLE

"Sometimes you will never know the value of a moment until it becomes a memory."
—DR. SEUSS

"Ninety-nine percent of all failures come from people who have a habit of making excuses."
—GEORGE WASHINGTON CARVER

"The time is always right to do what is right."
—DR. MARTIN LUTHER KING, JR.

"You can never cross the ocean until you have the courage to lose sight of the shore."
—ANDRÉ GIDE

"Those who cannot change their minds cannot change anything."
—GEORGE BERNARD SHAW

Your Gifts to the World

May I be protector for those without one,
  A guide for all travelers on the way;
  May I be a bridge, a boat and a ship
For all who wish to cross [the water].

May I be an island for those who seek one
  And a lamp for those desiring light,
  May I be a bed for all who wish to rest
  And a slave for all who want a slave.

May I be a wishing jewel, a magic vase,
  Powerful mantras and great medicine,
  May I become a wish-fulfilling tree
  And a cow of plenty for the world
And the great elements such as earth,
  May I always support the life
  Of all the boundless creatures.

And until they pass away from pain
  May I also be the source of life
  For all the realms of varied beings
  That reach unto the ends of space.

—*Shantideva, India, 760 AD*

What Is Your Service to the World?

God,
I'm willing
to do your work.
Please
show me what it is.

—Tami Simon, Boulder, Colorado

Finding Courage to Face the Unknown

Tender and compassionate God, you are our steadfast
companion in the joyous times of our lives. When we rejoice,
you celebrate with us; when we are anxious and afraid, you
offer us a relationship where we can find courage to face
the unknown; when we weep with sadness, you are our
comforter. Help us believe that you receive us as we are,
and help us to entrust ourselves, with all our many struggles
and hopes, to your faithful and abiding care.
Amen.

—Author Unknown

Tomorrow Is a New Day

Finish each day and be done with it.
You have done what you could.
Some blunders and absurdities no doubt crept in;
forget them as soon as you can.
Tomorrow is a new day.
You shall begin it serenely
and with too high a spirit to be
encumbered with your old nonsense.

—*Ralph Waldo Emerson*

Great Spirit

O Great Spirit
Help me always
to speak the truth quietly,
to listen with an open mind
when others speak,
and to remember the peace
that may be found in silence.

—*Cherokee Prayer*

Lord, Be with Us

Lord, be with us this day,
Within us to purify us;
Above us to draw us up;
Beneath us to sustain us;
Before us to lead us;
Behind us to restrain us;
Around us to protect us.

—*St. Patrick*

It's All Right There at Your Fingertips

And then I realized
that to be
more alive
I had to
be less
afraid
so
I did it…
I lost my
fear
and gained
my whole life.

—*Author Unknown*

The Right Thing

Doing the right thing is our best gift
That is what brings us bliss and happiness.
Happy and blissful is the person who does what is right,
because it is the right thing to do.

—The Ashem Vohu Prayer, Zoroastrian tradition

Do with Me What You Will

Father, I abandon myself into your hands;
do with me what you will.
Whatever you may do, I thank you:
I am ready for all, I accept all.
Let only your will be done in me,
and in all Your creatures—
I wish no more than this, O Lord.

Into your hands I commend my soul;
I offer it to you with all the love of my heart,
for I love you Lord,
and so need to give myself,
to surrender myself into your hands,
without reserve,
and with boundless confidence,
For you are my Father.

—Charles de Foucald

Have Patience

Have patience with everything unresolved in your heart
and try to love the questions themselves…
Don't search for the answers,
which could not be given to you now,
because you would not be able to live them.
And the point is to live *everything*.
Live the questions now.
Perhaps then, someday far in the future,
you will gradually, without even noticing it,
live your way into the answer.

—*Rainer Maria Rilke*

The Fall of the Leaf

The lazy mist hangs from the brow of the hill,
Concealing the course of the dark-winding rill;
How languid the scenes, late so sprightly, appear!
As Autumn to Winter resigns the pale year.

The forests are leafless, the meadows are brown,
And all the gay foppery of summer is flown:
Apart let me wander, apart let me muse,
How quick Time is flying, how keen Fate pursues!

How long I have liv'd—but how much liv'd in vain,
How little of life's scanty span may remain,
What aspects old Time in his progress has worn,
What ties cruel Fate, in my bosom has torn.

How foolish, or worse, till our summit is gain'd!
And downward, how weaken'd, how darken'd, how pain'd!
Life is not worth having with all it can give—
For something beyond it poor man sure must live.

—*Robert Burns*

To Think of Time: Part I

To think of time—of all that retrospection,
To think of today, and the ages continued henceforward.
Have you guess'd you yourself would not continue?
Have you dreaded these earth-beetles?
Have you fear'd the future would be nothing to you?
Is today nothing? is the beginningless past nothing?
If the future is nothing they are just as surely nothing.
To think that the sun rose in the east—
that men and women were
flexible, real, alive—that every thing was alive,
To think that you and I did not see, feel, think, nor
bear our part,
To think that we are now here and bear our part.

—*Walt Whitman*

October

O hushed October morning mild,
Thy leaves have ripened to the fall;
Tomorrow's wind, if it be wild,
Should waste them all.
The crows above the forest call;
Tomorrow they may form and go.
O hushed October morning mild,
Begin the hours of this day slow,
Make the day seem to us less brief.
Hearts not averse to being beguiled,
Beguile us in the way you know;
Release one leaf at break of day;
At noon release another leaf;
One from our trees, one far away;
Retard the sun with gentle mist;
Enchant the land with amethyst.
Slow, slow!
For the grapes' sake, if they were all,
Whose leaves already are burnt with frost,
Whose clustered fruit must else be lost—
For the grapes' sake along the wall.

—*Robert Frost*

If

If you can keep your head when all about you
  Are losing theirs and blaming it on you;
If you can trust yourself when all men doubt you,
  But make allowance for their doubting too:
If you can wait and not be tired by waiting,
  Or, being lied about, don't deal in lies,
  Or being hated, don't give way to hating,
And yet don't look too good, nor talk too wise;

If you can dream—and not make dreams your master;
If you can think—and not make thoughts your aim,
  If you can meet with Triumph and Disaster
  And treat those two impostors just the same:
If you can bear to hear the truth you've spoken
  Twisted by knaves to make a trap for fools,
  Or watch the things you gave your life to, broken,
And stoop and build 'em up with worn-out tools;

If you can make one heap of all your winnings
  And risk it on one turn of pitch-and-toss,
And lose, and start again at your beginnings,
  And never breathe a word about your loss:
If you can force your heart and nerve and sinew
  To serve your turn long after they are gone,
  And so hold on when there is nothing in you
Except the Will which says to them: "Hold on!"

If you can talk with crowds and keep your virtue,
  Or walk with Kings—nor lose the common touch,
If neither foes nor loving friends can hurt you,
  If all men count with you, but none too much:
  If you can fill the unforgiving minute
  With sixty seconds' worth of distance run,

Yours is the Earth and everything that's in it,
And—which is more—you'll be a Man, my son!

—*Rudyard Kipling*

Reflection

Reflect upon your present
blessings—of which every man
has many—not on your
past misfortunes, of which
all men have some.

—*Charles Dickens*

An Autumn Walk

Adown the track that skirts the shallow stream
I wandered with blank mind; a bypath drew
My aimless steps aside, and, ere I knew,
The forest closed around me like a dream.
The gold-strewn sward, the horizontal gleam
Of the low sun, pouring its splendors through
The far-withdrawing vistas, filled the view,
And everlasting beauty was supreme.

I knew not past or future; 'twas a mood
Transcending time and taking in the whole.
I was both young and old; my lost childhood,
Years yet unlived, were gathered round one goal;
And death was there familiar. Long I stood,
And in eternity renewed my soul.

—*W.M. MacKeracher*

Teach Me to Be Generous

Dearest Lord, teach me to be generous,
teach me to serve you as I should,
to give and not to count the cost,
to fight and not to heed the wounds,
to toil and not to seek for rest,
to labour and ask not for reward,
save that of knowing that I do your most holy will.

—*St. Ignatius of Loyola, sixteenth century*

Give Over Thine Own Willing

Give over thine own willing;
give over thine own running;
give over thine own desiring
to know or to be anything;
and sink down to the seed
which God sows in the heart,
and let that grow in thee,
and be in thee,
and breathe in thee,
and act in thee,
and thou shalt find by sweet experience
that the Lord knows that,
and loves and owns that,
and will lead it to
the inheritance of life,
which is its portion.

—*Isaac Penington, Quaker tradition (1661)*

Love in Autumn

I sought among the drifting leaves,
The golden leaves that once were green,
To see if Love were hiding there
And peeping out between.

For through the silver showers of May
And through the summer's heavy heat,
In vain I sought his golden head
And light, fast-flying feet.

Perhaps when all the world is bare
And cruel winter holds the land,
The Love that finds no place to hide
Will run and catch my hand.

I shall not care to have him then,
I shall be bitter and a-cold
It grows too late for frolicking
When all the world is old.

Then little hiding Love, come forth,
Come forth before the autumn goes,
And let us seek through ruined paths
The garden's last red rose.

—*Sara Teasdale*

Accepted

You are no longer young,
Nor are you very old.
There are homes where those belong.
You know you do not fit
When you observe the cold
Stares of those who sit

In bath-chairs or the park
(A stick, then, at their side)
Or find yourself in the dark
And see the lovers who,
In love and in their stride,
Don't even notice you.

This is a time to begin
Your life. It could be new.
The sheer not fitting in
With the old who envy you
And the young who want to win,
Not knowing false from true,

Means you have liberty
Denied to their extremes.
At last now you can be
What the old cannot recall
And the young long for in dreams,
Yet still include them all.

—*Elizabeth Jennings*

Live with Intention

Live with intention. Walk to the edge. Listen hard. Practice wellness. Play with abandon. Laugh. Choose with no regret. Appreciate your friends. Continue to learn. Do what you love. Live as if this is all there is.

—*Mary Anne Radmacher, from Live With Intention*

Take Control

Take control of your destiny.
Believe in yourself.
Ignore those who try to discourage you.
Avoid negative sources, people, places, things and habits.
Don't give up and don't give in.

—*Wanda Hope Carter*

Autumn

The thistledown's flying, though the winds are all still,
On the green grass now lying, now mounting the hill,
The spring from the fountain now boils like a pot;
Through stones past the counting it bubbles red-hot.

The ground parched and cracked is like overbaked bread,
The greensward all wracked is, bents dried up and dead.
The fallow fields glitter like water indeed,
And gossamers twitter, flung from weed unto weed.

Hill-tops like hot iron glitter bright in the sun,
And the rivers we're eying burn to gold as they run;
Burning hot is the ground, liquid gold is the air;
Whoever looks round sees Eternity there.

—John Clare

Shades of Gold

So many shades of gold
Autumn
Another miracle we take for granted
Another expression of the artist's vision
The blending of the autumn hues
with the setting sun
Warm
Comforting
Perfect
Thank you for autumn, Lord.

—John Birch

Grant Us This Day

Grant us, O Lord,
this day to walk with you as Father,
to trust you as Savior,
to be enlightened by you as Spirit,
to worship you as Lord:
that all our works may praise you
and our lives may give you glory.
Amen.

—*Anonymous*

Breathe in Us

Breathe in us, O Holy Spirit,
that our thoughts, our ideas, our words, may all be holy.
Act in us, O Holy Spirit,
that our works, our labors, our actions,
our living of life too, may be holy.
Embrace our hearts, O Holy Spirit,
that we may love and be love in a holy way.
Strengthen us, O Holy Spirit,
that our lives may represent all that is life-giving and holy.
Protect us, O Holy Spirit,
that we always may be your gifts of hope and life in this world.
Amen!

—*Saint Augustine*

When My Soul Findeth Wings

Like roses the bright dream did pass,
On swift, noiseless footsteps away;
Like glistening dew on the grass,
Dissolving beneath the sun's ray.

Like voice of the lark that doth soar,
Through the golden haze of the dawn;
You hear it and bend to adore,
Just hear it and then it is gone.

The lark on his swift, flashing wings,
Keeps pace with the flowers in their flight;
And that's why when soaring he sings,
And passes so swiftly from sight.

I slept, and a vision did see,
Of eyes that were tender and blue;
I awoke to know that for me
The vision may never come true.

The lark soars no more in the skies,
He's gone with the roses and dew;
The face with the soft tender eyes,
Comes never to gladden my view.

My memory holds images fair,
Of all these beautiful things;
Which I will be seeking somewhere,
When my soul, as lark, findeth wings.

—Libbie C. Baer

God, I Offer Myself to Thee

God, I offer myself to Thee—
to build with me
and to do with me as Thou wilt.
Relieve me of the bondage of self,
that I may better do Thy will.
Take away my difficulties,
that victory over them may bear witness
to those I would help of Thy Power,
Thy Love, and Thy Way of life.
May I do Thy will always!

—*Alcoholics Anonymous, Big Book, Third Step Prayer, 1939*

Wisdom, Strength, Light, Mercy

Give me, O Lord,
purity of lips,
a clean and innocent heart,
humility, fortitude, patience.
Give me the Spirit of wisdom and understanding,
the Spirit of counsel and might,
the Spirit of knowledge and godliness,
and of fear of the Lord.
Make me always seek your face with all my heart,
all my soul, all my mind.
Give me a contrite and humble heart in your presence.
Most high, eternal and holy Wisdom,
drive away from me the darkness
of blindness and ignorance.

Most high and eternal Strength, deliver me.
Most high and eternal Light, illuminate me.
Most high and infinite Mercy, have mercy on me.
Amen.

—Gallican Sacramentary

Never Stop Learning

Anyone who stops learning is old, whether at twenty or eighty.
Anyone who keeps learning stays young.
The greatest thing in life is to keep your mind young.

—Henry Ford

A Different Man

No man ever steps in the same river twice,
for it's not the same river and he's not the same man.

—Heraclitus

November

A Time to Give Thanks

"When you are grateful, fear disappears
and abundance appears."

—TONY ROBBINS

"Gratitude and esteem are good foundations of affection."

—JANE AUSTEN

"Wear gratitude like a cloak, and it will
feed every corner of your life."

—JALAL AL-DIN RUMI

"Gratitude is not only the greatest of
virtues, but the parent of all others."

—MARCUS TULLIUS CICERO

"I would maintain that thanks are the highest form of
thought, and that gratitude is happiness doubled by wonder."

—G.K. CHESTERTON

"Blessed are those that can give without
remembering and receive without forgetting."

—UNKNOWN

Start Your Day with Thankfulness

When you arise in the morning,
give thanks for the morning light,
for your life and strength.

Give thanks for your food, and the joy of living.

If you see no reason for giving thanks, the fault lies
with yourself.

—Tecumseh, Shawnee Chief

Give Us This Day

Give us this day
Which art in heaven,
Hallowed be
Your holy name.
Thy Kingdom come,
Just let your will be done
On earth,
As it is in heaven.
Give us this day
Our daily bread.
Forgive us our debts,
As we forgive our debtors.
And lead us not
Into all temptation,
But deliver us He said,
I am Safe
Safe

I am Safe
Safe
Safe
Safe
Safe
Safe
Hallelujah
Hallelujah
Hallelujah
Hallelujah
I'm safe.

—Ruth Baxter, with passage adapted from Luke 11:2–4

The Buddha's Guide to Gratitude

Give thanks
For what has been given to you,
However little.
Be pure, never falter.

—Buddha

There Is Enough for Everybody

May all be fed.
May all be healed.
May all be loved.

—John Robbins, 2002

Give Thanks for This Day and Every Day

Creator, open our hearts
to peace and healing between all people.

Creator, open our hearts
to provide and protect for all children of the earth.

Creator, open our hearts
to respect for the earth, and all the gifts of the earth.

Creator, open our hearts
to end exclusion, violence, and fear among all.

Thank you for the gifts of this day and every day.

—*Native American Chant*

Counting Our Blessings Every Day

For the expanding grandeur of creation, worlds known and
unknown, galaxies beyond galaxies, filling us with awe and
challenging our imaginations:
We give thanks this day.

For this fragile planet earth,
its times and tides, its sunsets and seasons:
We give thanks this day.

For the joy of human life,
its wonders and surprises, its hopes and achievements:
We give thanks this day.

For high hopes and noble causes, for faith
without fanaticism, for
understanding of views not shared:
We give thanks this day.

For all who have labored and suffered for a fairer
world, who have
lived so that others might live in dignity and freedom:
We give thanks this day.

For human liberty and sacred rites; for
opportunities to change
and grow, to affirm and choose:
We give thanks this day.

We pray that we may live not by our fears but
by our hopes, not by
our words but by our deeds.
We give thanks this day.

—*O. Eugene Pickett*

❧

Give Thanks Each and Every Day

To our Gods of old, we bless the ground
that you tread in search of our freedom!

We bless your presence in our lives and in our hearts!

Take of this offering to your delight,
and be filled with our prayers of thanksgiving!

May our lives remain as full as our hearts on this day!

—*Yoruban Grace*

Blessing for the Daily Meal

Thank you, God, for food so good,
and help us do the things we should.
Help us with our work and play,
and everything we do and say.
Amen.

—Author Unknown

Thank You for Making This World

Goodnight God.
I hope you are having
a good time being the world.
I like the world very much
I'm glad you made the plants
and trees survive with the
rain and summers.
When summer is nearly near
the leaves begin to fall.
I hope you have a good time
being the world.
I like how God feels around
everyone in the world.
God, I am very happy that
I live on you.
Your arms clasp around the world.

—Louise Baxter

Let That Word Be: Thanks

Better
than if there were thousands
of meaningless words is
one
meaningful
word
that on hearing
brings peace.
Better
than if there were thousands
of meaningless verses is
one
meaningful
verse
that on hearing
brings peace.
And better than chanting hundreds
of meaningless verses is
one
Dhamma-saying
that on hearing
brings peace.

—*Dhammapada, VIII, attributed to Buddha*

A Grateful Heart

God has two dwellings;
one in heaven,
and the other in a meek
and thankful heart.

—Izaak Walton

Cultivate Gratitude

Cultivate the habit of being grateful for every good thing
that comes to you, and give thanks continuously. And
because all things have contributed to your advancement,
you should include all things in your gratitude.

—Ralph Waldo Emerson

Hold On

Hold on to what is good
Even if it is a handful of earth
Hold on to what you believe
Even if it is a tree that stands by itself
Hold on to what you must do
Even if it is a long way from here
Hold on to life
Even if it is easier to let go
Hold on to my hand
Even if I have gone away from you

—Pueblo Indian Prayer

A Birthday

My heart is like a singing bird
Whose nest is in a water'd shoot;
My heart is like an apple-tree
Whose boughs are bent with thickset fruit;
My heart is like a rainbow shell
That paddles in a halcyon sea;
My heart is gladder than all these
Because my love is come to me.
Raise me a dais of silk and down;
Hang it with vair and purple dyes;
Carve it in doves and pomegranates,
And peacocks with a hundred eyes;
Work it in gold and silver grapes,
In leaves and silver fleurs-de-lys;
Because the birthday of my life
Is come, my love is come to me.

—*Christina Georgina Rossetti*

Prayer of Thanksgiving

We thank you, O God for your love for us.
Love that reaches out to accept us, wherever we are,
whoever we are.
Love that demands a lot, but at the same time, somehow,
amazingly, enables us to meet those demands.
Love that reassures, affirms, prompts, challenges, and
overwhelms us
with the completeness of its response.
Help us, your people, held within the security of your love, to
risk showing that same love to others.
May our love, too, be known for its abundance, its readiness to
speak out, and its healing power.

—Presbyterian church of Aotearoa, New Zealand

May God Bless Us

May God the Father who made us bless us.
May God the Son send his healing among us.
May God the Holy Spirit move within us and
give us eyes to see with, ears to hear with,
and hands that your work might be done.
May we walk and preach the word of God to all.
May the angel of peace watch over us and
lead us at last by God's grace to the kingdom.

—Prayer of St. Dominic

A Prayer of Thanks

Throughout all generations we will render thanks unto Thee
And declare Thy praise,
Evening, morning, and noon,
For our lives which are in Thy care,
For our souls which are in Thy keeping
For thy miracles which we witness daily,
And for Thy wondrous deeds and blessings toward us at
all times.

—Jewish Prayer

Bedtime Prayer

Father, we thank thee for the night,
and for the pleasant morning light;
for rest and food and loving care,
and all that makes the day so fair.

Help us to do the things we should,
to be to others kind and good;
in all we do, in work or play,
to grow more loving every day.

—Rebecca Weston (1890)

Meditation, May 11, 1661

My thankful heart with glorying tongue
Shall celebrate Thy name,
Who hath restored, redeemed, recured
From sickness, death, and pain.

I cried, Thou seem'st to make some stay,
I sought more earnestly
And in due time Thou succour'st me
And sent'st me help from high.

Lord, whilst my fleeting time shall last,
Thy goodness let me tell,
And new experience I have gained
My future doubts repel.

An humble, faithful life, O Lord,
Forever let me walk;
Let my obedience testify
My praise lies not in talk.

Accept, O Lord, my simple mite,
For more I cannot give.
What Thou bestow'st I shall restore,
For of thine alms I live.

—*Anne Bradstreet (1661)*

The Thankful Heart

The unthankful heart discovers
no mercies; but the thankful
heart will find, in every hour, some
heavenly blessings.

—*Henry Ward Beecher*

Gratitude

Gratitude unlocks the fullness of life. It turns what
we have into enough, and more. It turns denial into
acceptance, chaos to order, confusion to clarity. It
can turn a meal into a feast, a house into a home, a
stranger into a friend. Gratitude makes sense of our
past, brings peace for today, and creates
a vision for tomorrow.

—*Melody Beattie*

Contentment and Joy

An amazing thing happens when
you get honest with yourself and
start doing what you love,
what makes you happy.
You stop wishing for the weekend.
You stop merely looking forward to special events.
You begin to live
in each moment
and you start feeling
like a human being.
You just ride the wave that is life,
with this feeling of
contentment and joy.
You move fluidly,
steadily,
calm
and grateful.
A veil is lifted,
and a whole new perspective
is born.

—*Author Unknown*

Let Gratitude

Let gratitude be the pillow upon which you kneel to
say your nightly prayer. And let faith be the bridge you
build to overcome evil and welcome good.

—*Maya Angelou*

We Thank You for Your Presence

When the journey
through each day
becomes a struggle,
and we wonder
how much further
there is to go,
your gentle voice
can still be heard:
'Sit where you are,
for I am there,
rest once more
in my embrace.'
For your presence
along life's road,
wherever we might be,
we thank you, Lord.

—*Author Unknown*

Life

A crust of bread and a corner to sleep in,
A minute to smile and an hour to weep in,
A pint of joy to a peck of trouble,
And never a laugh but the moans come double;
And that is life!
A crust and a corner that love makes precious,
With a smile to warm and the tears to refresh us;
And joy seems sweeter when cares come after,
And a moan is the finest of foils for laughter;
And that is life!

—*Paul Laurence Dunbar*

We Are Thankful

We are thankful for this day that you have given us,
for its blessings, its opportunities, its challenges.
May we appreciate and use each day that comes to us.
We pray for strength and guidance for each day as it comes,
for each day's duties, for each day's problems.
May we be challenged to give our best always,
And may we be assured of your presence with us.
Amen.

—*Unknown*

The Importance of Gratitude

It is just that we should be grateful,
not only to those with whose views we may agree,
but also to those who have expressed more superficial views;
for these also contributed something
by developing before us the powers of thought.

—Aristotle

Worry Less, Praise More

We would worry less if we praised more.
Thanksgiving is the enemy of discontent and dissatisfaction.

—H.A. Ironside

Live by Your Words

As we express our gratitude, we must never forget that the
highest appreciation is not to utter words, but to live by them.

—John F. Kennedy

The Best Prayer

Thank you is the best prayer that anyone could say.
I say that one a lot. Thank you expresses extreme gratitude,
humility, understanding.

—Alice Walker

December

Joy to the World

"Appreciation is a wonderful thing. It makes what is excellent in others belong to us as well."

—VOLTAIRE

"To get full value of a joy, you must have someone to divide it with."

—MARK TWAIN, 1897

"There is no happiness like that of being loved by your fellow creatures and feeling that your presence is an addition to their comfort."

—CHARLOTTE BRONTË

"We can only be said to be alive in those moments when our hearts are conscious of our treasures."

—THORNTON WILDER

"Joy is the simplest form of gratitude."

—KARL BARTH

"Where there is love, there is joy."

—MOTHER TERESA

Perfect Be Our Unity

Let us be united;
Let us speak in harmony;
Let our minds apprehend alike.
Common be our prayer,
Common be the end of our assembly;
Common be our resolution;
Common be our deliberations.
Alike be our feelings;
Unified be our hearts;
Common be our intentions;
Perfect be our unity.

—*The Rig-Veda*

Sink into Joy

Flowers, sesame-seed, bowls of fresh water, a tuft of
kusha grass,
all this altar paraphernalia is not needed
by someone who takes the teacher's words in
and honestly lives them.
Full of longing in meditation,
one sinks into a joy that is free of any impulse to act,
and will never enter a human birth again.

—*Lalia, 1381*

In the Light of Each Day

In the joy of your heart,
Your light remains

In the gift of your caring,
Your light remains

Where you reached out to help,
Your light remains

Where you sat in silent peace,
Your light remains

In the place where you worked,
Your light remains

In the stillness of the starry night,
Your light remains

In the light of each day fully embraced,
Your light remains

Like the touch of an Angel,
Your light remains

When you live as a light,
Your heart is joined in the Infinite Light of Love.
And that about you which is eternal…remains.

—Reverend Jacquie Riker

The Joy in a Heart that Beats

Peace.
Peace, She says to me.
Peace to your soul.
I am the beauty in the leaf.
I am the echo in a baby's laugh.
I am your mother.
I am the joy in the heart that beats.
I am the free woman.
I am the one who breaks the shackles of oppression.
You are my hands and feet.

—*Gaian Prayer*

Where There Is Sadness, Let There Be Joy

Lord, make me an instrument of Thy peace;
where there is hatred, let me sow love;
where there is injury, pardon;
where there is doubt, faith;
where there is despair, hope;
where there is darkness, light;
and where there is sadness, joy.
O Divine Master,
grant that I may not so much seek to
be consoled as to console;
to be understood, as to understand;
to be loved, as to love;

for it is in giving that we receive,
it is in pardoning that we are pardoned,
and it is in dying that we are born to eternal life.
Amen.

—St. Francis of Assisi

We Are Reborn

O Holy Child of Bethlehem,
descend to us, we pray;
Cast out our sin, and enter in,
be born in us today.

—Phillips Brooks, 1867

Peace and Love

We do not want riches
but we do want to train
our children right.
Riches would do us no good.
We could not take them
with us to the other world.
We do not want riches.
We want peace and love.

—Chief Red Cloud, Oglala Lakota

Blessing of the Earth

It is lovely indeed, it is lovely indeed.
I, I am the spirit within the earth...
The feet of the earth are my feet...
The legs of the earth are my legs...
The bodily strength of the earth is my strength...
The thoughts of the earth are my thoughts...
The voice of the earth is my voice...
The feather of the earth is my feather...
All that belongs to the earth belongs to me...
All that surrounds the earth surrounds me...
I, I am the sacred words of the earth...
It is lovely indeed, it is lovely indeed.

—*Navajo Song*

Traditional Buddhist Prayer

May all beings have happiness,
and the causes of happiness.
May all be free from sorrow,
and the causes of sorrow.
May all beings never be separated
from the sacred happiness
which is sorrowless;
And may all live in equanimity,
without too much attachment
and too much aversion,
And live believing in the equality
of all that lives.

—*Buddhist Prayer*

Leave the World A Little Bit Better

To laugh often and much;
To win the respect of intelligent people
and the affection of children;
To earn the appreciation of honest critics
and endure the betrayal of false friends;
To appreciate beauty,
to find the best in others;
To leave the world a bit better,
whether by a healthy child,
a garden patch,
or a redeemed social condition;
To know even one life has
breathed easier
because you have lived.
This is to have succeeded.

—*Author Unknown, after the writing of Ralph Waldo Emerson*

Joy of Discovery

The joy of discovery
that moment
when hope and expectation
were gloriously met
by the illumination of one bright star.
We cannot imagine
what words were spoken by visitors
or if first impressions
left them somewhat confused.

Messiah, Savior, a King
born in the barest of palaces.
Yet they saw and fell down
on their knees in adoration.
Lord, they saw you and knew
whom they had met.
As we meet around crib
candle or advent wreath
draw us into that stable
in our imagination.

In the quiet moments of prayer
this Christmas, that brief oasis
from the bustle of the world
bring alive to us
the smell of the hay
the sound of the animals
the cry of a baby.

Draw us close to our Savior
Messiah and King as we bring

not Gold, Myrrh or Frankincense
but the gift of our lives
the only offering we can bring.

—*Celtic Prayer*

Glory Be

Glory be to the Father,
and to the Son,
and to the Holy Spirit.
As it was in the beginning, is now,
and ever shall be,
world without end.

—*The Gloria Patri*

Make a Joyful Noise unto the Lord

Make a joyful noise unto the Lord, all ye lands.
Serve the Lord with gladness;
come before his presence with singing.
Know ye that the Lord he is God;
it is he that hath made us, and not we ourselves;
we are his people, and the sheep of his pasture.
Enter into his gates with thanksgiving,
and into his courts with praise;
be thankful unto him, and bless his name.
For the Lord is good; his mercy is everlasting;
and his truth endureth to all generations.

—*Psalm 100*

His Peace Will Guard Your Hearts

Always be full of joy in the lord.
I say it again—rejoice!

Let everyone see that you are considerate in all you do.
Remember the Lord is coming soon.

Don't worry about anything,
instead pray about everything.
Tell God what you need,
and thank him for all he has done.

If you do this, you will experience God's peace,
which is far more wonderful
than the human mind can understand.
His peace will guard your hearts and minds
as you live in Christ Jesus.

—Philippians 4:4–7

Welcome Morning

There is joy in all:
in the hair I brush each morning,
in the Cannon towel, newly washed,
that I rub my body with each morning,
in the chapel of eggs I cook
each morning,
in the outcry from the kettle
that heats my coffee
each morning,

in the spoon and the chair
that cry "hello there, Anne,"
each morning,
in the godhead of the table
that I set my silver, plate, cup upon
each morning.

All this is God,
right here in my pea-green house
each morning
and I mean,
though often forget,
to give thanks,
to faint down by the kitchen table
in a prayer of rejoicing
as the holy birds at the kitchen window
peck into their marriage of seeds.

So while I think of it,
let me paint a thank you on my palm
for this God, this laughter of the morning,
lest it go unspoken.

The joy that isn't shared, I've heard,
dies young.

—*Anne Sexton*

Nearer to Thee

Nearer, my God, to thee,
E'en though a cross it be
That raiseth me,
Still all my song shall be,
Nearer, my God, to thee.
Nearer to thee!

—Louisa May Alcott

The Splendor of Eternal Light

May the Lord Jesus Christ,
who is the splendor of eternal Light,
remove from your hearts
the darkness of night. Amen.

May he drive far from you
the snares of the crafty enemy,
and always give you
his angel of light
to guard you. Amen.

That you may rise to your morning praises,
kept safe in him,
in whom is all
the fullness of your salvation.
Amen.

—Attributed to Mozarabic Psalter, eighth century

How Happy Is the Little Stone

How happy is the little Stone
That rambles in the Road alone,
And doesn't care about Careers
And Exigencies never fears—
Whose Coat of elemental Brown
A passing Universe put on,
And independent as the Sun
Associates or glows alone,
Fulfilling absolute Decree
In casual simplicity—

—*Emily Dickinson*

Joy and Gladness

Blessed are you, O Lord,
for you have nourished me from my youth
and you give food to all flesh.
Fill our hearts with joy and gladness
that we always have sufficiency in all things,
and may abound to every good work
in Christ Jesus our Lord;
through him be glory to you,
honor, might, majesty, and dominion,
forever and ever.
Amen.

—*Apostolic Constitution*

Late Fragment

And did you get what
you wanted from this life, even so?
I did.
And what did you want?
To call myself beloved, to feel myself
        beloved on the earth.

—*Raymond Carver*

The Right Blessings

O Lord our God,
teach us to ask you for the right blessings.
Steer the vessel of our life toward yourself,
the tranquil haven of all storm-tossed souls.
Show us the course we should go.
Renew a willing spirit within us.
Let your Spirit curb our wayward senses
and guide and empower us to our true good,
to keep your laws,
and in all we do always rejoice in your glorious,
        joyful presence;
for yours is the glory and praise from all your saints
forever and ever.
Amen.

—*St. Basil of Caesarea*

Happiness Is Like a Butterfly

Happiness is like a butterfly;
the more you chase it, the more it will elude you;
but if you turn your attention to other things,
it will come and sit softly on your shoulder.

—*after an 1848 definition of happiness in New
Orleans'* Daily Crescent *newspaper*

Giving Joy to the Heart

The precepts of the Lord are right,
giving joy to the heart.
The commands of the Lord are radiant,
giving light to the eyes.

—*Psalm 19:8*

To These I Commit My Day

Love. Joy. Peace. Patience. Kindness.
Goodness. Faithfulness. Gentleness, and self-control.
To these, I commit my day.

—*Anonymous*

You Make Us Glad

O God,
you make us glad
with the yearly expectation
of the birthday of Christ,
your only Son.
Grant that we,
who hail him with joy
as our Redeemer,
may also behold him without fear
when he comes to be our Judge;
through Jesus Christ our Lord.

—*Gelasian Sacramentary*

Life

Let me but live my life from year to year,
With forward face and unreluctant soul;
Not hurrying to, nor turning from the goal;
Not mourning for the things that disappear
In the dim past, nor holding back in fear
From what the future veils; but with a whole
And happy heart, that pays its toll
To Youth and Age, and travels on with cheer.
So let the way wind up the hill or down,
O'er rough or smooth, the journey will be joy:

Still seeking what I sought when but a boy,
New friendship, high adventure, and a crown,
My heart will keep the courage of the quest,
And hope the road's last turn will be the best.

—*Henry Van Dyke*

The Holy Night

We sate among the stalls at Bethlehem;
The dumb kine from their fodder turning them,
Softened their horned faces
To almost human gazes
Toward the newly Born:
The simple shepherds from the star-lit brooks
Brought their visionary looks,
As yet in their astonished hearing rung
The strange sweet angel-tongue:
The magi of the East, in sandals worn,
Knelt reverent, sweeping round,
With long pale beards, their gifts upon the ground,
The incense, myrrh, and gold
These baby hands were impotent to hold:
So let all earthlies and celestials wait
Upon thy royal state.
Sleep, sleep, my kingly One!

—*Elizabeth Barrett Browning*

The New Birth

'Tis a new life—thoughts move not as they did
With slow uncertain steps across my mind,
In thronging haste fast pressing on they bid
The portals open to the viewless wind
That comes not save when in the dust is laid
The crown of pride that gilds each mortal brow,
And from before man's vision melting fade
The heavens and earth—their walls are falling now—
Fast crowding on, each thought asks utterance strong;
Storm-lifted waves swift rushing to the shore,
On from the sea they send their shouts along,
Back through the cave-worn rocks their thunders roar;
And I a child of God by Christ made free
Start from death's slumbers to Eternity.

—*Jones Very*

Reborn Each Day

The world is new each morning—that is God's gift,
and a man should believe he is reborn each day.

—*Israel Ben Eliezer*

Sacred Joy

From joy I came,
For joy I live,
And in Thy sacred joy
I shall melt again.

—*Paramahansa Yogananda*

My Soul Is Greater Than the World

This morning my soul is greater than the world
since it possesses You, You whom
heaven and earth do not contain.

—*Saint Margaret of Cortona*

Dance for Joy

May all things move and be moved in me
and know and be known in me
May all creation
dance for joy within me.

—*Chinook Psalter*

When the Mind Is Pure

We are shaped by our thoughts;
we become what we think.
When the mind ia thing of bes pure,
Joy follows like a shadow that never leaves.

—*Buddha*

The Infallible Sign

Joy is the infallible sign of the presence of God.

—*Pierre Teilhard de Chardin*

Epilogue

Sharing the Blessings, Creating a Prayer Circle

In closing, I want to share with you one last way that you can express all of this newfound calm, and that is by creating a "Prayer and Blessings Circle." The idea is simple. A gratitude circle is a place for counting blessings and sharing stories, photos, prayers of serenity, and videos with friends and loved ones. The more people you can get to align with you, the sooner you will discover the positive power of gratitude and reap the many benefits that come from doing so. Now, we want to spread that gift and help you become cheerleaders for others who have tapped into the power of thankfulness by forming your own Prayer Circle. Connect with others in a special group dedicated to honoring the simple phrases, "Thank you" and "I am grateful for…" We know firsthand that once you start a thankfulness circle, it won't take long for others to join in, and the power of gratefulness will permeate and bless your everyday being. I want to share with you my tips for starting a circle, but first, I want to offer a few thoughts on what the world is going through as I write this.

We are more in need of mutual support than even before. In times when it is not always possible to be together for reasons of safety and healthy, it is an excellent idea to have these prayer circles over Zoom or Skype or whatever online service works for you. I started one every Wednesday entitled Heart Wisdom. At first, I worried if anyone would come and fretted needlessly; but after three weeks, something wonderful happened in a completely organic way. Everyone started to talk about what helped them get through the pandemic, sharing coping mechanisms and how to get through lonely days and weeks of sheltering in place. It has now grown to a regular group of folks from every walk of life and every age demographic. One of the most important aspects of this is that we had people also speak to what they were needing; one young woman spoke of struggling with depression and was met with encouragement, prayers, and volunteers checking in on her afterward. Another attendee shared that her grandfather had just died, and we were able to offer virtual hugs and much love and heartfelt care.

These prayer circles and zoom get togethers can become very important for connection, compassion, and in other ways one might never be able to predict. What I do know is that they will deepen your spirituality and illuminate your life for years to come. Here are my tips on starting a circle:

1. **Organize.** As the organizer, consider yourself the host or hostess, almost as if you have invited a group of friends—or people you hope will become friends— to your dinner table. Your role is to help guide conversations and serve up a feast (of interesting stories

about gratitude or nuggets of information to share) that will keep the conversations meaningful, inspiring, and ultimately bring to life the power of gratitude in all the lives of those gathered in your circle.

2. **Create a Mission or Goals for Your Circle**. What do you want to accomplish? How will you manifest gratitude in your own life and the lives of those in your circle? Will you share stories, inspiring quotes, guided meditations? Create a plan for guiding your group through the practice of gratitude.

3. **Decide Whether to Meet Online or In Person**. The exciting thing about the Internet is that you can create a Circle and community online and connect friends and colleagues from across the country—and the world. Or you may want to create an in-person circle with friends in your neighborhood or town.

4. **Make Connections**. Send out evites and invites and make phone calls to invite members to your circle. Ask everyone to invite a friend and spread the word about your new group.

5. **Select a Meet-Up Place**. Often guides will invite in-person communities to meet at their home. Or you may opt for a local coffee shop or a comfortable meeting place where you can gather regularly.

6. **Schedule**. Create a calendar of meet-up dates and distribute it to your group.

7. **Create Materials**. In this book we have lots of prompts and prayers as well as meditations and exercises to try. Please feel free to tap into these as resources.

8. **Talk About It**. Spread the good news about what being thankful can do as it manifests in your life and the lives of your friends, family, and members of your circle.

Circles of Grace

Those simple suggestions should help you and your circle get started. Remember, nothing is cast in stone, and you can feel free to improvise until you find your comfort zone. We guarantee you will come away from these gatherings feeling inspired, challenged, and with exciting new ideas to share.

First, begin by welcoming your guests. Go around the circle with each person introducing themself; for example, "I am Mary Smith and I live in Ohio. I am a writer, literacy volunteer, and mother of two." Next, read a passage of poetry, prayer, or prose. Now, go clockwise around the circle, and ask each participant why she or he is here and what spiritual sustenance he or she is seeking.

Ask a volunteer to read her favorite prayer or quote about being thankful. These group gatherings are wonderful, but personal sharing and goal discussion can be intimidating at first, so be mindful of your group and you'll sense when you will need to wrap things up. Always end on a high note by asking each person to share gratitude. May your transformation be your inspiration!

About the Author

Becca Anderson comes from a long line of preachers and teachers from Ohio and Kentucky. The teacher side of her family led her to become a woman's studies scholar and the author of *The Book of Awesome Women*. An avid collector of meditations, prayers, and blessings, she helps run a "Gratitude and Grace Circle" that meets monthly at homes, churches, and bookstores in the San Francisco Bay Area, where she currently resides. Becca Anderson credits her spiritual practice with helping her recover from cancer and wants to share this with anyone who is facing difficulty in their life.

Author of *Think Happy to Stay Happy* and *Every Day Thankful*, Becca Anderson shares her inspirational writings and suggested acts of kindness at: thedailyinspoblog.wordpress.com

Index of
Authors and Subjects

B

N

O

P

Q

T

U

V

W

Y

Z

Mango Publishing, established in 2014, publishes an eclectic list of books by diverse authors—both new and established voices—on topics ranging from business, personal growth, women's empowerment, LGBTQ studies, health, and spirituality to history, popular culture, time management, decluttering, lifestyle, mental wellness, aging, and sustainable living. We were recently named 2019 *and* 2020's #1 fastest growing independent publisher by *Publishers Weekly*. Our success is driven by our main goal, which is to publish high quality books that will entertain readers as well as make a positive difference in their lives.

Our readers are our most important resource; we value your input, suggestions, and ideas. We'd love to hear from you—after all, we are publishing books for you!

Please stay in touch with us and follow us at:

Facebook: Mango Publishing
Twitter: @MangoPublishing
Instagram: @MangoPublishing
LinkedIn: Mango Publishing
Pinterest: Mango Publishing
Newsletter: mangopublishinggroup.com/newsletter

Join us on Mango's journey to reinvent publishing, one book at a time.